Broken to Blended

Encouragement for Blended Families

Samara Leigh Ashley

Cover Design by Angela Hunt

Editing by Robert Powers

Photo Copyright maxphotography@istockphoto.com

ISBN-13: 978-0692307502

ISBN-10: 0692307508

I DEDICATE BROKEN TO BLENDED TO MY HUSBAND,

Through all of the joys and struggles of blending our family, one thing will never change: I am blessed to have you along this journey with me and my love for you grows with each passing day. Thank you for being not only my best friend, but my greatest supporter in all I do. I love you.

FOREWORD

Few books have captured my heart while reinforcing the truths of the Bible like Broken to Blended. Samara's straightforward approach compels the reader to venture beyond the safe waters of family normalcy, and dive into the exciting though turbulent seas of blending a family together.

Samara's wonderfully written narrative overflows with Godly wisdom and practical common sense that places you right inside the house—dirty laundry and all! You soon discover that your situation is not unique, and more importantly, you are not alone . . . God is walking with you through every treacherous chapter.

Writing from the experiences of her tragedies and triumphs affords Samara a perspective that offers readers insights into challenges experienced by blended families. Sage advice such as your spouse being a higher priority than your children (since most second marriages end in divorce), and relenting the title of "super hero" and "control freak" are Biblical precepts that often are ignored by authors.

Samara's devotions are saliently transparent and brutally honest. A classic example is the discussion of the multiple parents and grandparents discussed in, Day 24: The Not-So-Hallmark-Holidays. It's the stuff nobody wants to talk about but everybody is thinking! Her transparency is paralleled with writing that reflects a humble sensitivity rather than a vengeful anger. The outcome is a vision of the unmistakable hand of God right in the middle of her storm (See, Day 18: Life as a Soap Opera).

As one who was a widower with two children who was blessed to remarry, Broken to Blended is not just another story. It's my story as well. And, I suspect this is the story for so many voiceless folks who think they're in this squall alone and no one else could possibly relate. And then, right in the middle of the storm comes Samara, paddling a lifeboat through the choppy seas, reminding us gently though firmly that there is freedom from your past, and that God loves using the awkward, the unusual and the difficult for His glory.

Dear reader, grab hold of this wonderful devotional and don't let go until God has etched indelibly upon your heart the truths that with Him, all things are possible, and that His Son makes all things new!

Rick Rigsby, Ph. D.
Pastor, Motivational Speaker, Corporate Trainer
Author of *Lessons From a Third Grade Dropout*

INTRODUCTION
BROKEN TO BLENDED

We all know that raising a family and being a parent are difficult shoes to fill but, when you add the complexity of a blended family, it takes life to a new level. Whether it was a result of death of a spouse, divorce, adoption, children outside of marriage, or any other means; we are all in the same boat. We are trying to find the best way to raise our families in unity and love.

I don't know about you, but there have been times when I just didn't know if it would get any easier. I doubted my abilities as a mother and even, at times, as a "good" wife. I think we have such unrealistic expectations starting out that forces the feelings of defeat on us. Well, I know that I am a work in progress, and you are too, but with God all things are possible!

I pray that the words God has given me

will lift your spirits and allow you to KNOW that God has a perfect plan. If we continue to try and run this rat race alone; that's exactly how we will feel...alone. I'm here to give encouragement and hope. So, let's see what God wants us to learn along this journey together! Are you with me?

DAY 1 – LORD HELP ME!

Psalm 55:22 Cast your cares on the LORD and he will sustain you; he will never let the righteous be shaken.

There are those days that go by so smoothly, then there are the days when I'm crying out to God for help. As a parent, I'm sure you can relate. The days when you feel completely helpless or lost as a mom or dad. It's too bad we aren't programmed to keep from failing. I can think of some days when the kids are behaved, the house is clean, dinner is on the table, completed a day at work without messing up, and things are running smoothly.

Then there are other days...you know what I mean. Well, I've come to realize that if my focus is diverted, my entire day gets thrown off track. So many people have asked me, "How do you do it all?" By "all," I'm assuming they mean work a full-time job, manage five kids, somehow keep up with chores, and still look like I've got it all together. Well, the answer isn't clear.

You see, I don't feel like I've got it together all of the time! But, I know that God will not give me more than I can handle so I keep moving forward.

Did you read the verse above? I mean, really focus in on what it says? Cast ALL your cares on the Lord and He will sustain YOU. What an awesome promise and hope. This, people, is how I make it through some rough days.

We will be getting into more specific details later, but this is the core. If you don't start your day with God, then you are just cruising along without any sense of direction.

How are we supposed to raise our family and keep it together on our own? We are not! We can't! We can try all we want to keep things together, but sometimes it just gets overwhelming.

So, first step for a smoother transition is to prioritize your walk with the Lord. Start your day refreshed and renewed! Whether blended family or not, married, single, divorced, widowed, or just starting life out on your own...this is for you!

If you don't know what in the world I mean when talking about God or daily time with Him, I would be so happy to share with you. This is the reason I live life with a smile!

If you have already started your day today without this time, get on it tomorrow. Make it a priority! Get your spouse involved with you or just find a place of solitude where you can think quietly.

Thoughts for the day:

1. What makes me the most frustrated during my day?

_____

_____

_____

_____

2. Have I asked God to help me in this area of my life? _____

3. When will I give God time each day?

_____

4. When was the last time I opened my Bible?

_____

5. Commit to making time with God each day for the next week. Can you do this?

_____

Prayer:

Lord, You know that I cannot do everything on my own, but I'm constantly trying to take control. I pray that You will give me the peace and clarity of mind to make it through my day. When I get frustrated, I pray that You will remind me of all I am blessed with. I thank you for the roof over my head, my spouse, beautiful healthy children, _____ (add your blessings). I know with You, God, all things ARE possible! Amen!

DAY 2 GOD BLESS OUR BROKEN ROAD

Psalm 25:5 Guide me in your truth and teach me, for you are God my Savior, and my hope is in you all day long.

I can remember back when I first met my husband, Steve. I was so excited and nervous at the same time. I had been through a very tough life change and here I was raising my two young girls.

I had come to a place where I felt at peace about my current situation, raising my girls as a single mom. The Lord had done a lot with me in a short time and I was resting in His loving arms. Little did I know that He had other plans coming my way.

Steve also had two young children and was living in the same shoes. I remember the day like it was yesterday. I was working at a local pediatrician's office. The ladies that I worked with had been haggling me about this guy I knew nothing about. They were trying to make a love connection, but I was just not ready for it.

I remember one day, my friend Pam came down the hall to get me. She kept talking about this guy, Steve, and I just couldn't make a connection. Then, there was the moment.

Standing face to face, I could feel my face turning bright red. He smiled, and of course, I smiled back. After all, for those that know me, there is usually a permanent smile on my face. Can anyone say "awkward?"

Well, this man would bring his son in for shots and, eventually, we said a few words. After a while, he asked me to a concert. I replied with a friendly "no." I just wasn't ready.

Bless his heart, he didn't know what he was getting into. After all, here I was with two little girls and what felt like a train wreck of a life at the time.

Some time passed and I did end up giving him my number and email. But, I wasn't going to let my guard down that fast. After all, I had decided that there were a lot of questions I was going to ask this time around. These questions were going to be tough for anyone to answer, but I felt that if I was going to get into another relationship, I owed it to myself to "investigate." Poor Steve!

For 3 months, I pretty much interrogated him with all kinds of questions. I told him at any point if he felt uncomfortable or didn't think this is what he wanted, then it wouldn't hurt my feelings. Well, after 3 months of "questioning," not only from me, but all the ladies surrounding me (yes, I know it sounds terrible), Steve and I were official.

Then you ask, how do you date with kids? When do you introduce someone to your children? Well, I'm no expert, but I will tell you how we did it.

First of all, my parents always taught me that you "date your future mate." This doesn't change just because you've been married before. I truly believe you should only date those you potentially see as a partner for life. Not simply date for companionship to keep from loneliness.

So, we dated with all four kids 95 percent of the time. The other 5 percent we would go out on our own. I told Steve along with my parents, if it didn't work dating with four kids, then it surely wouldn't work being married with four kids.

As for Steve and I, we had no reserves about the kids meeting each other and knowing what was happening. We were very comfortable with that decision. If either of us had doubts, we wouldn't have done it this way.

From that point on, I fell madly in love with Steve. My family loved him and his family took me and the girls in as their own. In June 2008, we were married. My dad is a pastor, so it was so nice to have a simple family wedding in my parent's living room.

Surrounded by all of those who loved us through the toughest times, we said our vows. We had a special part of the wedding for the kids. We gave them each a special gift to show them how much they meant to us. We had a family prayer where we asked God to mold us as one. Well, that prayer has continued ever since.

You may be wondering why I am sharing all of my personal life with you. Do I have to? No, but I told the Lord a long time ago.... I knew He didn't desire for me to be a divorced single mom. But, through it all, I have an incredible journey to share with others.

I can't tell you how many times the Lord has put people in my path that I could encourage through hard times. Did I always have the right words to say? Nope! At times I was clueless. But even if I could give some kind of hope and encouragement I was going to do it.

I'm a very open person. Some may say I'm too transparent, but I don't want to hide my past and pretend it never existed. I believe I'm where I am now for a reason. I believe God has bigger plans to use my story and if that's the case I will "shout it from the mountaintops."

So, for today, where are you with your family or relationship? Are you already married? About to merge families? Worried about how your children will do with a step-parent situation? Let's reflect back to the above verse. Psalm 25:5 "Guide me in your truth and teach me, for you are God my Savior, and my hope is in you all day long." It's time to let God have the reigns and we need to allow Him to show us what we are to do.

Thoughts for today:

1. It's time to think back on your relationship with your spouse/boyfriend and how it first started. Take some time to recall your own story. Look how far you've come! Write down a few obstacles

you have overcome along the way.

_____

_____

_____

_____

_____

_____

2. Think about your life. Not your spouses or
someone else you know, but your own! What
situations in your own life can you let God use for
His glory?

_____

_____

_____

_____

_____

_____

3. Are you willing to let God use you?

_____

4. Have you come to a place where you are willing
to be transparent for the sake of
others? _____

Prayer:

Lord, I pray that I will never forget where I have
come from. You have pulled me from the miry
clay and set my feet upon the rock. I praise you,
Lord, for bringing me through life's struggles. I
know that it will not always be easy, but I trust

You to direct my life. I pray for my spouse and my children today. I pray that You will protect and keep our family in Your hands. I pray that You will walk us through this life on earth and help us to make wise choices. I love you Lord! Amen!

DAY 3 - WHEN TWO PATHS CROSS

Colossians 1:10-12 so that you may live a life worthy of the Lord and please him in every way: bearing fruit in every good work, growing in the knowledge of God, being strengthened with all power according to his glorious might so that you may have great endurance and patience, and giving joyful thanks to the Father, who has qualified you to share in the inheritance of his holy people in the kingdom of light.

And so it began...first came love, then marriage. I remember our honeymoon was a little out of the ordinary. First, we had to make sure all the kids were dropped off to their other folks before we could sneak away. We were gone for two days and then I don't think either us knew exactly what we were in for.

It's like the feeling of being a parent for the first

time again, except more complicated. There were schedules we had to keep up with, along with shipping kids from one place to another. Not ideal, but we made it work. It wasn't until a few months later that we experienced our first meltdown. It was the tantrum that I wasn't prepared for.

That's when I figured out how much different mine and Steve's parenting styles were. Steve had been single longer than I before we got together. He had more of a laid back parenting style than I did. Kids slept with him, no bedtimes, eat on the run. Whatever he had to do to survive life as a single dad, he did it the best he knew how. His mom took over the mother role for the kids for years, so they saw her more as a mother figure. Steve shared custody so his weeks were split. He was used to having no children around half the time, so he had some time for himself.

I, on the other hand, had primary custody of the girls. I had them with me most of the time. I was able to keep consistency with bed times, family meals, and structure. I can't take all of the credit though, I had a lot of help from my mom and sister. I was taught that consistency was the key to raising a family and it was so helpful during my transition. It wasn't what I thought my life would be, but I would make it work.

But now, here I was trying to love and be loved by two kids that were not mine. As much as I would love to tell you it was an easy transition, it just was not. I think I had a harder time emotionally than anyone else.

Things would be fine for the time we had the

kids, but as soon as they would come back from time away, it took an entire day for them to adjust back to a routine. This is a good place to share a friendly tip. You can only keep a routine at your own home. No one else will agree to raise the kids the way you do.

So, if you are at this point, it's time to hand it over to God. I stressed so much as a Christian mom having to send the kids off to living situations I was not comfortable with. But, again I had to hand the control over to God.

You say, God already has control? Yes, I know that, but my human self continues to take over. It's still a struggle today.

This was the beginning of many conversations. Maybe not the most fun talks, but when you merge into a family unit you each have to give it one hundred percent and talk it through no matter how difficult.

Well, it was difficult. It was hard to tell my husband that I didn't agree with giving into the kids whenever they had a meltdown and on the other end, he thought I was too strict. Both of us felt we were doing the right thing.

In reality, there was nothing wrong with either style. We just had to figure it all out together. When you have been on your own, you are not used to having someone tell you what they think. It's a hard thing to swallow.

Let's look at the verse above. Did you notice the part about how you can "be strengthened with all power according to his glorious might so that you may have great endurance and patience?" That's exactly what the doctor ordered! I needed the kind of strength, endurance, and patience that only came for the Lord.

Believe me, I'm definitely still a work in progress. You know that old song, "He's still working on me, to make me what I ought to be." However, I also like to say, I'm not who I want to be, but praise God I'm not what I used to be!

Thoughts for today:

So what stage are you in today? Are you struggling as I did (and still do at times)? Let's talk it out for a minute.

1. First, let's break down the two parenting styles. You first. Be honest. Do you have a routine? Rules or boundaries you feel strongly about? Make a list of the most important things to you regarding the kid's upbringing. Now your spouse/partner. What is their parenting style?

_____

_____

_____

_____

_____

_____

2. What are your biggest frustrations with parenting?

_____

_____

_____

3. Have you shared your feelings? How did it turn out?

_____

_____

_____

_____

4. Here is the hard part. Have you considered trying a different way other than the "my way or the highway" concept? It's time to start thinking as the parents and not the single parent mindset that you came from.

One thing I know, change is constant! The more you talk it out, the better it can be for everyone.

Prayer:

Lord, you know my heart and that my intentions are only for the good. I pray today that my relationship will continue to be made strong even through the struggles we face. I'm so thankful, Lord, for the marriage you have given me. I pray that you will give us guidance as we raise our kids together. Lord, you know I get frustrated and at times emotional, but I give it all to you. I can't do it without Your help. I trust You with my kids and my spouse and know that You want the best for us. Thank you for never leaving my side! Please allow me to start fresh tomorrow with a new mindset. Amen.

DAY 4 - LOOKING FOR ANSWERS

Psalm 126:2-3 Our mouths were filled with laughter, our tongues with songs of joy. Then it was said among the nations, "The Lord has done great things for them." The Lord has done great things for us, and we are filled with joy.

Have you ever needed direction and turned to a self-help book? Well, I needed some help. Steve could see I was struggling with the constant reminder that I was raising someone else's kids. I was a step-mom. I never really liked the name. After all, every time I heard the word it reminded me of Cinderella's evil step-mother.

At first, the kids called me mom, but it didn't last long. Too many people were telling them what to do or not to do. I could tell it was confusing them. Remember, unless there are no other parents involved, you may have the same issues.

I recall the frustration of going out with my family, whether it be to a restaurant or the mall, and someone say, "Are these all your kids?" Of course, I would reply with a "yes" because they were "our" kids. But then, one would say "she is not my mommy" or "I have another daddy." Then I would feel the need to explain my life story! How draining! Have you been there? Are you with me people? I didn't want to have to constantly walk that emotional road with complete strangers, but I didn't want people to judge me.

I've been on the opposite side. Growing up I had so many friends divorce. I never thought that could possibly be me! I know the thoughts that ran through my head at the time, "I wonder what they did to break up their marriage?" Now, there I was living life as "one of those people." Obviously, I have grown to be a more compassionate person because of this.

So, I started reading these books Steve found for me in the local Christian bookstore. I will tell you now, I couldn't finish it. If I cried before I read them, I cried more after reading the first few chapters. Here I was just trying to treat everyone the same, yet to be continually told I was not mom. I just wanted to have a normal family!

Obviously, my mindset was not where it needed to be. My family was not the traditional family that God intended. We had been broken and then mended again together - blended. There was never going to be the sense of normalcy that I wanted and it was time I started to grasp that.

The book started telling me to realize that "I will never be their mom." Ok, I'll agree that the book wasn't wrong, it just felt brutal at that time. Honestly, I just didn't feel good about reading it. I never finished. I needed a little comic relief.

For those that know me, I like to be silly and laugh a lot. So, I decided to turn my frustrations into fun. We sat down, just me and the older kids, to come up with a "new name" they would like to call me since "mom" wasn't going to work out. Well, we came up with "sugar mama!"

I know it sounds crazy, but we had fun with it. You should have seen the look on people's faces when we would walk the aisles of the grocery store and one would say, "Sugar Mama, I want....." I could have rolled on the floor and laughed. It may sound strange, but to each his own! It worked.

From that point on, I could let go of my need to be called "mom" and just move forward. After all, it's just a name. It didn't change the fact that I loved them all as my own.

I remember one day, Terek (the oldest boy), decided he would like to start cooking with me. I love to cook and create my own recipes. So, we started cooking together.

That time was our bonding time that we shared at first with no one else. It's something we could do together to make him feel special. We would have great talks about the future and him becoming a young man all while we messed up the kitchen. It allowed me the time with him that I desired. Now, he called himself a "hit". Husband-in-training. I loved it! It's just so gratifying to see that all the time and energy were paying off.

So, now I have learned to fight the frustrations

with humor. No, it doesn't always work with certain situations, but it is a great way to relieve some stress.

Sometimes, I just decide to revert back to being a kid. That may mean practicing new wrestling moves with Terek or playing spa with the girls. Diverting my attention in the midst of a sometimes chaotic life is helpful.

So for today, rejoice in your hardships! Let there be joy in your home! How long has it been since you have just laughed to the point of tears? "The Lord has done great things for us" so we should be joyful.

Thoughts for today:

1. Have you struggled in your own parenting role? If you are a step parent, are you frustrated with the labels?

_____

_____

_____

2. What can you do to lose the stress and laugh a little? What are some things you can start teaching the kids that may interest them and give you the quality time you need together?

_____

_____

_____

_____

_____

_____

3. Again, it's a daily battle giving it all over to God, but you can do it. Write down 2 or 3 things that you are going to try and change in your household. Write down a plan of action and what you are going to replace it with.

_____

_____

_____

_____

_____

_____

Prayer:

Lord, you know my frustrations as a step parent. I know You did not intend it to be this way, but I pray today that You will use me to raise all the kids to know how much they are loved. Help me not to get frustrated and upset in front of them. Help me to be open with my spouse about how I am feeling. Lord, I come to You first asking for Your help and guidance. Sometimes this life feels so lonely and like no one else understands, but I know that You understand me. You made me and know the number of hairs on my head. I praise You, Lord, for what You are about to do in my life and in the life of my family. Give me a peace today. Amen.

DAY 5 TOO BLESSED TO BE STRESSED

Philippians 1:6 Being confident of this, that he who began a good work in you will carry it on to completion until the day of Jesus Christ.

When I was a little girl, I remember having bedtimes, curfews, house rules, and lots of structure. My mom, Stephanie, was a stay-at-home mom also raising a blended family of her own.

I can remember some nights crying about bed times. Later as a teen, I remember begging for more sleep. It's funny how a few years can change everything.

My mom also raised five children. She married into a family, then had the last three of us later on. She always told me how she couldn't have done it without a routine. I now can confess to this. There have been so many times where I have called her needing advice and she has always been willing to talk me through it.

Now, here I am in the exact same boat. Raising a blended family of my own. When Steve and I married, the kids were two, four, five, and seven. Luckily, young enough to be able to implement some kind of routine.

The children were already used to their "parent sharing" schedules. Terek and Jernee would split the week, while Hailey and Avery would only go every other weekend. The merging of the schedules took some adjustment.

For someone who didn't like a lot of change, I had to push through the challenges. I quickly realized that my marriage was not just going to be about Steve and me. I had to now share my life with the ex-spouses. I had to find a way to openly communicate with someone I did not know, which usually I find rather easy. It did not come as easy as I imagined.

I quickly felt like I was caught in the eye of a hurricane. I felt like the routine I was trying to create was quickly being crushed. I tried to implement bedtimes for all the kids equally. This didn't work. Terek had been staying up until 9pm at 7 years old. Despite my reserves, I couldn't change something he was used to. It wouldn't be fair to give him so much change in a short period of time.

There had to be an easier way for change without affecting the kids too much. The last thing I wanted was a negative reaction. So, his bedtime stayed at nine. Since the girls were so young, I was able to get them down earlier.

The purpose of the set bedtimes was to give

Steve and I some alone time. My top priority was my relationship with God, but my husband always came before the kids. That's how God intends it. How are we supposed to make it work if we don't communicate or have time alone?

With statistics showing that the majority of second marriages end in divorce, I am, and have always been, determined to make Steve a priority. So, there are many days where the kids go to the basement to play the Wii or go to their rooms to read. This time is spent with Steve. Sometimes we have things we need to talk over. Sometimes we just sit together and watch a favorite tv show, but either way we get some time in. We have dinner together and I try to cook as much as possible. The kids all chip in with housekeeping and chores.

These are just a few things we do to keep it all together. Do I have it all together? Really?! Is that a real question? No way!

There are many days where I don't even get to shower until the end of the day. I walk around with spit up stained clothes and disheveled hair. My house is "lived in," but clean. I've got about fourteen loads of laundry per week so if I miss a day the laundry room looks like a war zone.

All of this to say, I can't do it all. I'm not superwoman, but I am a real woman. I love my God, my man, and my kids. I do my best to keep up with it all, but fail miserably many times. However, I'm too blessed to be stressed so, I choose to keep moving!

Thoughts for today:

1. Write down your daily routine with your kids.
(Example: school, pick up, homework, dinner,
showers, bedtime) Maybe you don't have a
routine. Maybe it's time to rethink this! Why stress
yourself and rush everywhere? The time is now.
Make some notes, talk with your spouse, and get
them on board.

_____
_____
_____
_____
_____
_____

2. When can you and your spouse have at least 10
minutes together uninterrupted? Make your
partner a priority. The kids are fine without you
for 10 minutes. If you have a little one, be
creative. If you want to make time, you can.

_____
_____
_____

3. Remember, you are not a super hero. You
cannot do it all and should not be expected to. If
your kids are old enough to be helpful, let them
help. You do not have to ask, you are the parent.
If they don't learn how to do chores now, who
will teach them? Let's raise our kids with a good
work ethic. Write down a few things they could
help with. Only implement one chore at a time per
child.

_____

_____

_____

_____

_____

Prayer:

Thank you, God, for giving me a full quiver! I love my kids and just want to raise them knowing you. That is my first priority. Please help me to know how to relate with each child separately as I need to. Help me to implement some responsibility, so I don't feel so overwhelmed at times. Help me to be consistent in my parenting. Help my spouse and I to work as a team. Thank you for Your direction and guidance. Amen!

DAY 6 - BEING THANKFUL

1 Chronicles 16:34 Give thanks to the Lord, for he is good; his love endures forever.

1 Thessalonians 5:18 Give thanks in all circumstances; for this is God's will for you in Christ Jesus.

Do you know why there are two verses for today? Because, we often forget about thanking God for what He has done for us. Me included. I can go an entire day and complain or get upset, when, all the while, my blessings continue to grow around me. I'm so blinded by my own selfishness that I do not even see all the good unfolding.

I don't know about you, but I can't stand to be around someone who constantly complains. I despise it really. There is so much negativity today without us adding to it.

So why do we? I have a motto, "kill it with

kindness." I teach it to my kids almost daily. I'm honestly repeating it for myself, but it is good for them to hear as well. I know, "kill" is not a nice word, but you get the point. I don't want to be the kind of person no one wants to be around.

When I'm confronted by someone that only wants to complain, I try and turn it around. Killing it with kindness basically means you "redirect" to a positive.

For instance, I do this with myself all the time. I try to teach my kids to share, but when it comes to sharing my kids, I simply don't like it. But, what could be another scenario? What if I couldn't see them at all? What if I lost them? What if they were fighting a terrible illness? I know these are a lot of "what ifs," but it is real life! I think sometimes we don't think things could happen to us or our kids. However, life can take tragic turns.

So why do we dwell on all the negatives? It's time to change our thinking and get positive! You'd be so surprised by your family's reaction to your change of attitude.

It is so hard to let your kids go and then count down the days until their return. Sometimes, you may call multiple times and never get to talk to them while they are away. I remember when the girls were just one and three. I cried every time I had to drop them off. Avery was in diapers and didn't even talk yet. Hailey was testing all boundaries. I would come home and feel an immediate sense of loss. Yes, I knew they would be back in two days, but I did EVERYTHING for them. Previously, they had never been away from me. I couldn't even go to the bathroom alone!

I recall thinking to myself and wondering how things changed so fast. What did I do to deserve this life? I didn't want any of this! If I was going to survive this for the next eighteen years, I had to come up with a plan.

For now, I keep a busy schedule while they are gone or jump into a new DIY projects. Yes, I definitely watch HGTV and plan ahead for when they are away. It's my therapy!

Now, I have a new way of thinking. First of all, their dad has remarried and I really love his wife, Jennifer.

You know what I love? The fact that I don't have to worry about who will be the "mommy" when I'm not there. I know they will be fed, bathed, cared for, and, most of all, loved when they are gone.

I know some may think I'm crazy for saying this, but who wouldn't want their kids to have a happy transition? I had to put my self-centered feelings aside and concentrate on what was more important for the kids. Not easily done, but it is a start.

Sometimes you have to let your guard down. It took me three years to be "ok" with the way things changed. It doesn't happen overnight. Give yourself time, but stop being the center or the beginning of unnecessary arguments.

Thoughts for today:

1. Are you caught up in the negativity today? When was the last time you caught yourself

getting worked up over a situation you could not control? Write down your last negative comment you made about your personal situation.

_____

_____

_____

_____

_____

2. Now, pretend you are the one listening to the ranting and raving. Would you want to be around someone like that? Are the words you are saying glorifying to God? Or are you tearing someone else down for your own benefit? Maybe it makes you feel better about yourself? Or do you still feel miserable afterward?

_____

_____

_____

_____

3. It's time to put your selfishness aside and concentrate on what is real and what is important. What are the 5 top things you desire for your children? Examples may be safety, love, or security.

_____

_____

_____

_____

_____

4. Now, are they getting the things you listed

without being unrealistic? Do they come back home knowing they are loved and wanted? If so, what's the problem? We should be so grateful for our children's smooth sailing despite our past and how it has affected them. How are you going to turn your negativity to positivity? Write 3 things related to your actions and attitude that you will work on and stick to it.

_____

_____

_____

_____

_____

_____

Prayer:

Lord, I come to You today with a thankful heart. I'm so sorry for my behavior that I know has not been pleasing to You. I've had my focus off track and I pray You will give me the strength to change it. I'm a hot mess of a parent most days, but I know I can make it with Your help. I lay all of the frustrations and hurts at Your feet. I know I can be free in You. Please lift these burdens from me. You are the only one I can find joy and peace with. Help me not to look to others for the answers that I know can only be found in You. Thank you! Thank you! Thank you! I'm blessed beyond measure!

DAY 7 - GREAT OR SMALL HE LOVES THEM ALL

Matthew 6:33 But seek ye first the kingdom of God, and his righteousness; and all these things shall be added unto you.

How many kids do you all have together? Do you consider yourself a large family or a small? Whichever, God loves each one. I hear all of the time, people trying to talk others into more children. I always say "to each his own."

It is not our position to tell others how many kids they should have or not have. The Bible says to seek the Lord's direction first, not your best friends or family's!

Again, it's prioritizing as the Bible indicates. Why is it that we ask people when they will have a baby as soon as they marry? Why not give them a break and let them figure life out first?

I remember when I was trying to get pregnant. I

was so sure it would happen quickly with each one. Well, it didn't happen as quickly as I thought it should. I probably bought twenty-five pregnancy tests and would overwhelm myself. I didn't know any better! After all, I got pregnant with Hailey without even planning! I had the five year plan and, after three years, she arrived.

When people would ask me continually when I would have another, I just wanted to scream. I've had so many friends that could never have children and some that got pregnant many times, but lost their sweet little ones. It's time we give people some privacy and respect.

Growing your family is a personal decision. But, when adding to a blended family, which is already so complex, it is difficult. There are so many questions to ask yourself.

I had the following questions run through my mind:
~ Does my spouse want a baby with me?
~ How will the kids respond?
~ Can I handle another one?
~ Will the kids be jealous when they leave and the baby stays?

Here is our story... when Steve and I married, I already knew that we were not going to have any children of our own. He had already shared his thoughts on this. I knew about this going into the marriage and was fine with it. After all, I already had two beautiful girls and with the addition of another girl and a boy (FINALLY); I thought that would be enough to handle. Little did I know that my feelings would change.

After about a year of marriage, I began having a strong desire for a baby. Not just any baby, but Steve's baby. It was hard for me to have so much love for someone and not be able to experience such an amazing event with him. I longed for this.

I remember the first time I mentioned the thought to Steve. He laughed. You know, the nervous kind of laughter. He didn't know how else to react. I think it caught him off guard. He would remind me that he felt he was fine without any more kids. I shared my feelings, but they were not reciprocated. He just wasn't feeling the same way.

In the next year, God worked so much in our lives. Our spiritual lives had been tested over and over again, and through it, our relationship strengthened. At this point, I had decided to give up on the thought of another child. It hurt me to think that I would never have his child, but I respected his opinion.

When I surrendered control, God stepped in. I remember it was November 2010. Steve came home one day after church and said we needed to "have a talk." I don't like to hear those words.

We sat together in our room and he shared with me how he had felt like the Lord was changing his heart. I was in shock! I had finally let it go and now he was bringing it all back up again! I didn't know how to react. I wanted to yell out in excitement, but then I was also guarded. Why now? What changed?

Steve went on to share his heart with me. He felt like he was making the decision selfishly and never asked God to direct him. We sat there staring at each other wondering what was next. What if we tried and couldn't get pregnant? How would the kids react?

Then, a few months later, we decided to go to a friend's wedding in Florida where I grew up. I needed some distraction. The day we were leaving I had decided to take a test. I just felt different. Sure enough, we were pregnant!

I was shocked! I just couldn't believe it was real. Jumping ahead, now we have little Levi. His name says it all. It means "united or unity."

The kids you ask? They are elated! They are the best big siblings and love to play with him. We will talk more about the transition into all of that later, but for now I'm continuing to glorify God for this sweet little blessing.

Thoughts for today:

1. Do you have a big decision to make concerning adding on to your own family? Whether through pregnancy or adoption? Why not take your request straight to the One who knows all? Ask the Lord's guidance on your life and the life of your family.

_____
_____
_____

2. List your top 5 concerns about bringing another child into your family.

_____
_____
_____

3. How does your spouse feel about the decision? Are you both on board or is one not as comfortable with the idea? What about the kids?

_____

_____

_____

_____

_____

4. Last of all, seek he first the kingdom of God and His righteousness. Fervently pray that God would either swing that door wide open or slam it shut so you know His will. Be patient. Wait on the Lord. God timing is perfect!

Prayer:

Lord, I pray you will continue to lead our family in the direction You want us to go. Please help me place my wants aside and focus on Your wants. I'm so thankful for my spouse and awesome kids. I just want to be the parent you want me to be. I know I make mistakes every day, but You know the desires of my heart. I praise You today for whatever is to come. Thank you Lord for Your continued blessings! Amen!

DAY 8 - IN THE HOT SEAT

James 3:5-6, 8, 17 Even so the tongue is a little member, and boasteth great things. Behold, how great a matter a little fire kindleth! And the tongue is a fire, a world of iniquity: so is the tongue among our members, that it defileth the whole body, and setteth on fire the course of nature; and it is set on fire of hell. But the tongue can no man tame; it is an unruly evil, full of deadly poison. But the wisdom that is from above is first pure, then peaceable, gentle, and easy to be intreated, full of mercy and good fruits, without partiality, and without hypocrisy.

Have you ever had your children ask you questions you simply did not want to answer? Maybe it was "where do babies come from?" Or maybe they asked "what was the worst thing you ever did growing up?" Well, I can tell you that one of the hardest questions I've ever encountered was

"why are you and daddy not married anymore?"
And "what happened?"

Whew! I don't know about you, but those are some tough subjects. I made the decision long ago not to discuss the "reasons" why I divorced with my kids until they were grown adults. By then, if they are still asking we will discuss it.

Some may disagree, but let me put it simply. My kids have already been through enough and I don't need them having a negative impression of their parent. You never realize, until you have lived it, what children of divorced or single parents go through.

They have two homes, two sets of parents, different rules and structures at different houses. Some have to deal with painful emotions or separation. It's simply not fair. It all comes back to that decision made so many years ago.

In our case, the children were extremely young. They were not as emotional as a grown child may have been going through a parents divorce or death. They adjusted very well and continue to grow with the twisted sense of stability we give them.

I don't want to rehash or relive every detail of the road I traveled. It was a very emotional journey. I know that if I am supposed to share my story with them at a later time, God will direct that.

Let's get into the scripture for today. The tongue, you see, is a fire. Once you kindle a fire, it grows from there. It can get out of control quickly. Have you ever started venting to a friend and just got off on a tangent you didn't mean to bring up?

My point exactly! We are human! We are not self-controlled naturally! Why put yourself in a place to destroy your relationship? Not only with your ex, but with your spouse as well! Children need to be able to just be children. Care free and not worrying about what their parents think of each other!

Honestly, I don't care to know what people think of me. As long as I know that I'm living for the Lord and trying my hardest to please him, I will be less and less concerned about public scrutiny. Does gossip and aimless chatter hurt? Yes, but I try to aim my focus upward and cast my cares on Him.

What about you today? Can you control your tongue or do you like to sound off to anybody who will listen to your fiery speech? What's the purpose? Are you trying to make yourself look better?

Well, I can tell you it will only make you hate yourself in the end. So, how can you change? It's a daily struggle to control such a small portion of ourselves. But, maybe this will help.

Thoughts for today:

1. Read James 3. Yes, the entire chapter!!! Now, list 3 things it says about the tongue.

_____
_____
_____
_____
_____

2. Now comes the hard part. It's time to be brutally honest with ourselves. Does the majority of what comes out of your mouth lift up or tear down? This is not only about your family life, but in any area. Write down the top 3 things you are frequently mouthing off about.

_____

_____

_____

_____

_____

_____

_____

3. How can you control your tongue? With God, you can do all things! Give it up to Him. Confess your faults and frustrations. He is waiting for you to share your life with Him. So, what are you waiting for. Don't you want to have more joy? This is a great way to bring it all back. It's time to use that tongue for encouragement and praise. Write down 3 things you are going to use your words for. To name a few examples, praising your spouse in front of the kids, telling the kids how much you love them and are proud of them, redirecting negativity when it comes your way.

_____

_____

_____

_____

_____

_____

Prayer:

God, I have completely lost it when it comes to my tongue. I let my frustrations over power me and just let go of all self-control. I pray You will give me the tools I need to use my speech for only the things glorifying to You! I pray you will help me to respond to others the same way I would like to be talked to. Let me see the good in people and be more compassionate. I pray one day if my children want to know about my past that You would provide me with the right words to say. Help me to work on a better relationship with the other parents involved. I lay all of this at the foot of the cross today! Amen!

DAY 9 - WHAT'S LOVE GOT TO DO WITH IT

1 Corinthians 13:4-7 Love is patient and kind; love does not envy or boast; it is not arrogant or rude. It does not insist on its own way; it is not irritable or resentful; it does not rejoice at wrongdoing, but rejoices with the truth. Love bears all things, believes all things, hopes all things, endures all things.

How did your relationship begin? Did you spot your mate out somewhere? Was it a blind date? Did you grow up as friends?

I remember the first eye contact Steve and I had. We were in a pediatrician's office where I worked. Then, later, the look turned to a touch. It was actually by accident.

Terek, the oldest boy, would come to have his allergy shots. One day, he was having a hard time sitting still when I was attempting his shot. Steve and I both went to grab hold of him and our hands touched. (Cue the slow motion and romantic music)

Steve loves to tell his version of this story all the time. He says, "as soon as our hands touched, our eyes met and I knew that I was going to marry this woman!"

Yep! He called it! We have come so far from that point now. Marriage, many job changes, health crisis, financial burdens, new baby, and a call to the ministry have all occurred in a very short period of time.

How did we get through all of our trials? With God's love and with the continued love we have for each other.

You see, just because we came from divorce doesn't mean that we think of that as an option for our marriage. It is not even a thought in my mind. I don't use it as a tool for arguments such as "well then I will just leave!" I don't even like to say the "D" word.

I am determined to grow old with this sweet man of mine and him with me. We pour out innumerable hours together to nurture what we have.

Does that mean we don't ever disagree? No, my husband could tell you that I am not perfect. I get upset over petty things or some days I'm just in a "female funk" as I like to call it. But you know what? He loves me through it.

When we start to love God first and dedicate time to Him, we in return learn to love our spouses and ourselves more easily. God starts to peel away at our "ugliness" and starts to soften our hearts towards the feelings of others. It is so true! The more time I spend in the Word, the easier time I have treating my husband and kids the way they deserve.

If I am not open to asking God to show me my faults and help me work through them, then I am not working on securing my relationship. It's just like I'm standing there with a sign that says "I'm not the problem you are!" I'm pointing blame or fault to everyone, but the real source...ME!

So, my husband tries to put my desires before his and I place his needs or desires before mine. This way, we are both working towards the same goal. What's our goal? To love each other as the scriptures teach.

Part of our love for each other is putting our relationship before the children. It is also showing affection. Yes, we even kiss and hug in front of the kids! We usually get caught in the kitchen.

If you have one or more kids, you know that as soon as you get a second alone, their radar kicks in and begins setting off an alarm. Whether you go to your room for alone time or are just trying to talk quietly for a moment, it is bound to happen.

Our kids are a little different than most. They come in the kitchen and get a kick out of us kissing. Some kids get grossed out, but ours cheer us on.

Either way, it is healthy for them to see that you are in love. It builds stability and security for them and it gives me time with the one I love. So until God calls me home, I will continue to live every day reminding my spouse of how blessed I am to have him as my life partner.

Thoughts for today:

1. Write your story of when you first met. What connected you to each other? Write a few details of what attracted you to your spouse.

_____

_____

_____

_____

_____

_____

_____

2. Now, what are you doing to strengthen your marriage? Do you give your spouse praise? Do you help them around the house? Are you respectful to them in front of the children?

_____

_____

_____

_____

3. It's time to take focus off the kids and place it on your spouse. The kids will survive without 24/7 attention.

Actually, I believe it will be better for them. Let them see how much you love each other. Be affectionate to your spouse in front of the kids.

Here's your homework for this week. Take every opportunity today to show affection to your mate.

Sit down and give them your undivided attention for at least 10 minutes each day. Talk about life and your future goals.

Prayer:

Lord, I want to be a loving companion. I want to love and treat people how I want to be treated. Please work on my heart and allow me to be compassionate towards others. Help me to show love to my spouse every day and not take the time we have together for granted. I want my love to reflect I Corinthians 13. I pray that you will make me and mold me into the person You want me to be. Amen.

DAY 10 - WITHOUT WORDS

1 Thessalonians 5:17-18 Pray without ceasing. In everything give thanks: for this is the will of God in Christ Jesus concerning you.

Have you ever had a time in your life where you wanted to cry out to God, but you were so burdened that you didn't even know how to pray? Maybe life had taken some turns you weren't expecting with a loss of some sort? Did you or your spouse lose a job? Did you have a death in your family? Were you broke financially? We're you dealing with a rebellious child?

Whatever the situation, if you have had an extreme low in your life you can remember this feeling. It's a place where you feel drained physically, emotionally, and spiritually.

A few years ago, Steve was called into the ministry. He had a job working part-time at a local church doing youth ministry and was going to college part-time. I've been a nurse for thirteen years and have always been able to find some kind of work.

Everything in our lives seemed to be running smoothly. After all the life changes we had already been through, I was thankful for some consistency. We were at a church we loved; surrounded by people we called our family.

Then one day, Steve felt the Lord calling us away from our home church. I didn't understand. He had a great opportunity starting out in ministry and we had a great group of youth involved. What was I missing? He said he couldn't explain why God was telling him this, but that we needed to be obedient.

Wow! I felt an overwhelming sense of worry. I had never been the "worrying kind," but this surely brought it out in me. All I could do was pray and trust that he was listening to what God wanted for our family.

This change meant that we would be entering the unknown waters. I had grown up twenty-five years in the same church where my father pastored in Florida. I had to church hop after moving from home and remembered feeling a sense of loss. Here I was again without a church to call my own. For this gal, it was unsettling. So, we prayed.

Not only did it mean no church, but it also meant no job or income for Steve. We would be on one income and with the bills coming in from all sides, I was fearful. I've always been a financial planner. I had saved for moments like these, but even when you try your hardest you can't force money to grow on trees.

To add a little more intensity, this is the same time we found out we were pregnant with Levi. As I said the other day, God decides when the timing is perfect, not us.

As weeks and months passed, we continued to pray and seek God's will for our family. By this time, the bank accounts were about empty. Steve had told me before this adventure that he felt God would show us the way, but it may be when we had full reliance on Him for everything. I remember many days where I needed to get bread and milk and there was no money left. Steve would find me crying in my office at home. We would cry out to God for help. One day, Steve decided to go up on the mountain to pray. He seemed to do this a lot during this time. We were struggling to get by and he didn't know what else to do, but go talk to God.

While he was praying on that mountain, he got a phone call. It was an acquaintance of his that hadn't called him in years. He told Steve that God had put him on his heart and he wanted to meet him for lunch. Little did this guy know that we had no money for lunch.

Steve went. The man treated him to a meal and prayed with him. When they finished, he reached into his pocket, and pulled out a twenty dollar bill. He told Steve he felt God calling him to give this to him.

I remember this moment like it was yesterday. There I sat 6 months pregnant in my office crying to God for help. In walks Steve with tears rolling down his face. He had no words, but placed that money on my desk. I asked him where it came from and he shared the story with me. This was a true act of God!

I know this story is long, but it wouldn't be the same without a little more detail. The night before this occurrence, we were lying in bed discussing our fears. We wanted to pray together, but neither of us had words.

Scriptures began pouring through my heart and mind. I began to speak them out loud to Steve as I cried out to God. He would quote verses back to me. We went back and forth like this for what seemed like an hour. God's amazing peace began to swell in our hearts and we were able to rest that night knowing He was in complete control. God sent people in our lives the next few months that had the same calling from God. His timing was always perfect.

I can tell you today, there was no logical explanation why we didn't lose our home, have our power turned off, or how we were able to have food on the table. It was by God's amazing grace that we had exactly what we needed right when we needed it.

Thoughts for today:

1. Do you remember hitting a low point in your life? Did you feel like there would be no end? Write down your story and how God brought you through it. Or, if you are in the storm now, write it down.

_____

_____

_____

_____

_____

_____

_____

_____

2. Have you ever memorized scripture? It is amazing to me how God brings verses to my mind that I learned as a child. Start today! Memorize the verse above. When you call upon the Lord, He will give you what you need at just the right time. The Bible is His book to us! It's time we learn more about it!

3. Has God ever called you to help someone in need? Did you listen? I hope my story inspires you to be obedient to what He is asking of you today. Steve and I have felt this need for others as well and have been obedient even when we didn't have it to give. God will provide if you obey! If you feel God leading you, don't disregard his call.

_____

_____

_____

_____

Prayer:

Lord, You alone have brought me through some stormy waters. I am so thankful for you guiding me through _____ (name a difficult time in your life). God, I may not know what tomorrow brings, but I know that You know. I trust in you,

God, to guide my life and my family. Sometimes I don't feel I have words to pray, but I will continue to cry out to You and seek You through the storms of my life. Thank you for loving me. Thank you for Your grace and mercy! Amen.

DAY 11 - PARENTAL CONFUSION

Proverbs 22:6 Train up a child in the way he should go: and when he is old, he will not depart from it.

Have you ever had a moment where you just wanted to yell out "who is the parent here?" Or "does anyone ever discipline their kids anymore?" Not only have I experienced this myself, but I can go out in public and think that same thought over and over again.

I can tell you right now, my parents made sure we knew who was in charge in our home. I had a respect for them and sometimes a little fear depending on what I had done. Oh boy has that changed!

There are not many days that go by when I don't wonder what is going through parent's heads! When did it become the "child knows best" mentality? It's time Christian family values return

61

to the forefront.

As a blended family, we have many "hands in the pot" as I like to call it. Many different parents with different styles of parenting. As I mentioned before, Steve and I come from different parenting backgrounds. It took some adjustment to come together, but we make it work for us. We have to work at this daily because we seem to be hit with a decision often.

However, we also have to make it work with four other parent's involvement. Not only the ex-spouses, but their spouses as well since everyone has remarried. You may be thinking "man, that's a lot of people!" Yes! My thoughts exactly!

So, how do we make it work? We have to communicate with each other all the time. For example, if I don't let Steve know when I've disciplined one of the children for something, how can he support my decision if he doesn't have a clue?

If Steve is not home, he trusts me to handle the discipline. If I am not home I support Steve's decisions to discipline. But, what happens when they go back to the other parent's homes?

You see, others may not be consistent with discipline or they honestly may not care about certain behaviors as strongly. So, what can I do? I can work with Steve to come up with a solution for our home.

You can't expect the punishment to follow to another house if other parents are not supportive of it. I've decided to maintain my consistency amongst the inconsistency and to not get so upset when others do not respond to the kid's negative behaviors. Through lots of prayer and time with God, I continue to "press on toward the goal."

My goal is to do exactly what the verse above says. Train up our children in the way they should go.

What way is that? I want the kids to grow up knowing and loving the Lord, loving themselves, treating others with respect, and respecting their parents. I want my kids to learn responsibility and have a great work ethic.

I love watching my children grow. I love listening to their dreams and I can't wait to see what paths they decide to take.

The Bible talks about how children should obey their parents and how parents should discipline their kids. It doesn't say "parents let your children make their own decisions." I've seen children grow up starting "adult" behaviors very young.

Why are we allowing our children to make decisions beyond their years? That's why God has given them to us, so that we can direct them with God's help.

Now, I'm not talking about not letting little Johnny pick out what he wants to wear to school. I'm talking about the kids making plans without asking permission from the parent or being disrespectful yet still having all the privileges they had before.

In our home, computers, TV, cell phones, and toys are all luxuries. They aren't a must have and can be taken away if necessary.

Above all, I want God to tell me one day "Well done, my good and faithful servant." I have entrusted you with many children and you have followed my Word."

Believe me, I mess up many times over and over again. However, I also know that God can forgive me as well as my kids. I can pick myself up and keep trucking through this temporary life here on earth. So what about you?

Thoughts for today:

1. Do you let your children call the shots at home?

_____

Do you get respect or do you feel like you are the child a lot of times? Let's read a few verses together today. Read these scriptures and take a few notes about what they say: Proverbs 22:6 above.

_____

_____

Ephesians 6:1-3 Children, obey your parents in the Lord, for this is right. "Honor your father and mother"—which is the first commandment with a promise— "so that it may go well with you and that you may enjoy long life on the earth."

1 Timothy 3:4 He must manage his own family well and see that his children obey him, and he must do so in a manner worthy of full respect.

Colossians 3:20 Children, obey your parents in everything, for this pleases the Lord.

2. What are you teaching your children? Are they

going to grow up loving the Lord? Will they have a strong work ethic and know how to accept responsibility? What are 3 ways you can be teaching your children important life lessons?

_____

_____

_____

_____

_____

3. Finally, are you being the godly example that your kids need? If not, how can you expect them to succeed and mature as you desire them to without godly direction? It's time we get on our knees and pray for our children as they grow. It all starts today.

_____

_____

_____

_____

Prayer:

God, you know I have made so many mistakes as a parent. It seems sometimes like I have no clue what I am doing here. I pray that You will direct me and guide me to what I should be doing. Please help me raise our children to be strong, independent, motivated kids. I want them to love You, Lord. I know that starts with me. Please give me the strength to be consistent with discipline and structure for the kids. Please help me to remember that we are not perfect and we all make mistakes. Help me to show the kids Your loving mercy and Your unconditional love when things don't go as planned. With You, Lord, I can do all things. In Jesus name, Amen!

DAY 12 - WHY ME?

Romans 12:12, 14, 15 KJV
Rejoicing in hope; patient in tribulation; continuing instant in prayer; Bless them which persecute you: bless, and curse not. Rejoice with them that do rejoice, and weep with them that weep.

Have you ever felt like God was calling you to share your story or testimony with someone? You may have felt a strong sense of urgency to share.

What was your reaction to this? Did you simply push that thought aside thinking "what could I possibly say that would be helpful?" I've been there.

When you come from a traumatic event, whether it be from divorce, death of a family member, some type of abusive situation, or simply a difficult change in life, God can use you!

I've felt for a long time that God was going to

use my story for His glory. I didn't know what that meant, but not until recently did I feel like I could be more transparent. It's scary. You know, opening up your life to strangers. There may be times when you share with someone and you get a completely different reaction than what you were expecting. Don't let it stop you from what God has placed on your heart.

I remember back to the weakest point in my life. The low of all my lows. I had become a single mom. Wait!! How did this happen to me? I went into my marriage with nothing but thoughts of growing old together.

Then, there I was.... twenty-six and divorced with two young girls. I felt like the walls were caving in on me. My sense of stability was crushed. I cried out to God until I had no tears left to cry.

I went through the stages of anger, grief, and loss. It seemed like an endless path. Is this what I lived my life for? For this ending? I thought to myself "I did it all like I was supposed to!"

I loved God, loved my husband, my kids, and my family. Why? Why did this have to happen to me? I did not get an answer quickly.

I remember one day at my work there was someone who wanted to "keep her marriage alive." Everyone was sitting around giving great ideas for romance. I remember saying, "try being spontaneous and surprise him for a date."

I will never forget the response I got. "Well, obviously that didn't work for you!" Without being able to control myself, I burst into tears. How could anyone be so hurtful to someone going through a difficult time? Why would she say this?

It goes back to our human inability to control the tongue. Many people may judge you because of your past, but God is bigger than all of this.

Why stuff your past in a box? Look what you have made it through. Have you learned from your mistakes? Have you given this over to God? If so, He has already forgiven you! Why live the "woe is me" life, when He has got better plans for you?

I remind myself every day that God will handle the judgments from others. I can't control what others may say about me, but I can have the confidence that God has given me and go forth! I don't think I would be as strong of a person today had I not had to go through the trials.

Think about a blacksmith's job. What does it take to make a beautiful piece of art? It has to be heated in the fire and beaten with his tools as he perfects his piece. Think about how this relates to you. You are a work in progress! I am a work in progress!

God's not finished with us yet. He doesn't want you to have to endure more than you can handle and has promised that you won't have to. He also says, "I will never leave you nor forsake you."

Praise God for His promises! Please don't forget about your past. Weeping may endure for the night, but joy comes in the morning! Let God use you today!

Thoughts for today:

1. Write about your most difficult moment in your life. This may be emotional to do, but it is healing.

_____

_____

_____

_____

_____

_____

_____

2. Now, write about how God brought you through it. If you are still in the storm, write about someone who has been there for you along the way.

_____

_____

_____

_____

_____

_____

_____

3. Have you encountered someone recently who needs some encouragement of their own? Do you feel you can be transparent with them? Invite them for a cup of coffee and tell them how God has brought you through your storm. Be an encouragement to someone else today!

_____

_____

_____

Prayer:

God use me! Use my life as a living testimony to others! I want people to feel like they can talk to me about difficult times. I need Your strength, God, to be bold. I don't want to put my past in a box and pretend that wasn't a part of me. Please give me the discernment to know when someone is hurting. Help me to show love to everyone and not be judgmental. I will go where You lead me! Thank you for being there for me. Amen.

DAY 13 - THE RESULTS

2 Corinthians 9:6 But this I say, He which soweth sparingly shall reap also sparingly; and he which soweth bountifully shall reap also bountifully.

There have been times in my life when I have felt as if all of the sweat and tears of step-parenting would not pay off. As much as I tried to keep things running smoothly, there would always be bumps along the way.

I wanted so badly to love and be loved, but it simply takes time to build a new relationship. Regardless if you have dated months or years before merging your families, kids need time to adjust to all the life changes that have come their way.

When Steve and I married, we realized how important it was for each of us to spend extra time with the kids. I needed to get to know the older kids on a deeper level and the same with Steve and the younger two.

We took the kids on individual dates to spend quality time with them. We waded our way throughout different obstacles with each child.

My experience with Jernee (the oldest daughter) usually consisted of side hugs and friendly reminders that I was not her mom. As time went on, she began to relax knowing that I was not trying to take her mom's place. I remember one day, Jernee came to me after I got off work. In her hand was a handmade card. Little did I know that what I was about to read would bring incredible joy. On the front she had drawn a beautiful picture and on the inside she had shared her heart with me.

It read, "Dear Sami, you are the best step mom ever! You help me when I have problems or when I feel bad. You help me with my homework." That was it! What I wanted so badly. To know that the words I shared and the love I portrayed would finally begin paying off.

From that point on, I began receiving many hugs and kisses followed by an "I love you!" Then came the "Sami, can you tuck me in?"

Not to make Steve feel bad, but I would get so excited when I would be asked over Daddy. Of course, Steve loved it just as much. He could see the smile on my face and the joy flowing from my heart!

Now that we've made it over the hump, the initial hardships have passed. We have truly become a family in all aspects. The kids hate to be apart and we don't like a quiet house.

Most of my joy and frustrations come when we

are all under the same roof. The house can get to be a mess quickly, the kids run through the house like they are zoo animals, they have disagreements, but they are HOME!

I love what someone said to me last weekend. They said, "If you were to come to our house when our kids were growing up, you would probably find them swinging from the chandelier or jumping off the roof tops." Now, they hold tight to those insane moments and wish they could go back in time.

I'm so thankful to God for giving me such big hearted children. They love each other and show love to others in so many ways. They are each unique as God made them and I treasure each one.

Each child has a special way of showing love. Terek, the oldest, is just like Steve. He has a huge heart for others and will tell everyone how much he loves them. He has a heart for people that are hurting and is encouraging.

Jernee is tender-hearted. She is compassionate and very sensitive to others. She has a harder time saying "I love you," but when she says it you know she means it.

Hailey is the goofball. She loves to get tackled with a hug. If you try to give her a normal hug, it will be awkward. She is super smart and has a very easy time in school. She loves anything related to crafts and baking.

Avery is the cuddle bug. She loves to sit on Steve's lap and tell him he is loved. She will tell you the reasons why she loves you and has no problems showing affection. She is a little mommy and is so helpful with her little brother.

And of course, Levi is on the run. He will stop to give a slobbery kiss between car racing and playing ball. His nickname is "tornado" for a good reason. If you blink, he will be gone. He thinks he is as big as the other kids and talks like he is 10!

So, all in all, I have learned to be thankful for each little act of love I am given. We have come so far from the "merge." We are unified. We are one. We are family!

Thoughts for today:

1. What difficulties do you face with your step-kids?

_____
_____
_____
_____

Have you recently gotten married or have you been married now for years? _____

2. Write down character traits of each child.

_____
_____
_____
_____
_____

Now, write down how they respond best to you. Is it through encouraging or kind words? Is it through acts of love?

_____

_____

_____

_____

3. Be patient! Wait on the Lord! As you work to grow your relationship with your children and step-children remember that each child is different. They have different needs. We can't talk to each one the same and get the same responses. I encourage you to seek out ways your children respond best and put it into action.

Prayer:

Dear Lord, thank you for your unconditional love for me. Thank you for bringing my family together. I pray today you will help us to grow together in unity. I want the kids to be there for each other as they get older. I want the kids to know how loved and treasured they are. Please help me see what each child needs from us as parents. Help us to speak to them in their own love language. Help me not to be negative or condescending. I want nothing more than for the kids to grow up knowing they are loved and wanted. Thank you again for your faithfulness to us. We are so blessed! Amen!

DAY 14 - FINDING PEACE

Mark 4:37-40 And there arose a great storm of wind, and the waves beat into the ship, so that it was now full. And he was in the hinder part of the ship, asleep on a pillow: and they awake him, and say unto him, Master, carest thou not that we perish? And he arose, and rebuked the wind, and said unto the sea, Peace, be still. And the wind ceased, and there was a great calm.

Some days are filled with sports practice, homework, dinner, church, room cleaning, showers, and hopefully, bed as close to bed time as possible. For me included! You know those "hairy" days that you feel pulled in every direction; only to be hanging on by a thread! You can imagine with five kids, we have a lot of days like this. It's not even including my husband's schedule. As a pastor, he may be called out or have to take a call at any time. Luckily, this is routine for me growing up as a PK (Preacher's kid). It's not unusual for the kids and me to just pick up and go as we need to.

However, running around like a chicken does take its toll after a while. I am left with my tank running on empty and needing some time of my own. Can you relate? Some people have a lot more on their plates than I do. I try to put a limit on the number of activities we are involved in to keep my sanity.

There are days when things flow smoothly and then there are days when everyone is on edge and I have to "divide and conquer," as I like to call it. Sometimes, the kids get wild and dividing them up to their rooms makes all the difference. After about thirty minutes, the house is quiet again and they are "released" from their imprisonment.

During the down time, I am able to simply sit and refocus. I'm human and can get easily flustered. As a mom, I'm just trying to keep it all together, but I can't do it all. I have a great partner who supports me, but I still have to have my time with the Lord in order to keep me on track every day. I'm one of those who talks to God throughout my day. I simply call out to Him when I need clarity or calmness. You see, we can't get that on our own. We need Him to give us the strength and the patience to get through each day. Isn't it so nice to know that He doesn't expect us to walk this life on our own?

Sure, Steve could help me all he wants, but without God I'd still feel lost and frustrated. I can't depend on Steve for my happiness and my security! That comes from God. Yes, Steve makes me very happy and also makes me feel secure, but I can't put that pressure on him.

God is the only one who can bring true peace and contentment. So, let's start today by realizing that it only comes from our Creator. He is holding his arms out to you and waiting on you to call on Him today. How long will you make Him wait? How long has He been standing there with arms wide open?

Thoughts for today:

1. It's time to peel all of life's frustrations away one by one and place them at the foot of the cross. What happens if you were to put twenty layers of clothes on right now? You would get hot, uncomfortable, and maybe it would make it hard to breathe. So, why do you layer yourself with too much responsibility? God wants you to bring it to Him! Start to shed those layers today and visualize laying each burden at the foot of the cross.

2. Who are you relying on for your peace and happiness? If it is not God, then you will never truly be happy. Believe me, I've tried it. It doesn't work out! It's time to refocus on the one who created you! You are unique and special in your own way. He knows that and He wants to have part in your life. Sit down and just talk with Him for a few minutes.

3. Have you got your kids involved in way too many activities? Is it getting in the way of attending church and your walk with the Lord?

It's time to figure out what is really important to you. Do sports and activities help or hinder your life with God? How can you prioritize better and make sure that "busyness" is not interrupting your spiritual life. Write down all that you are involved in. It's time to redirect your focus today.

_____

_____

_____

_____

_____

_____

_____

Prayer:

Lord, thank you for being the calm in the storm. Thank you for giving me this verse today and reminding me that You are the One who is with me through all my life's struggles and all the joys. Today, may I bring glory to You in all I do and say. Help me to refocus on what this life is all about, You! Help me to take that time with You that I need every day. Lord, I want that peace and joy! I want people to see that You have made all the difference in my life. Bless my family today. Amen!

DAY 15 - GIVING YOUR ALL

Matthew 11:28-30 Come unto me, all ye that labour and are heavy laden, and I will give you rest. Take my yoke upon you, and learn of me; for I am meek and lowly in heart: and ye shall find rest unto your souls. For my yoke is easy, and my burden is light.

Have you ever been part of this scenario? From the moment you wake up until the second you put your head down, you have been running non-stop. It starts with the kids whining and not wanting to wake up or complaining about what clothes they have laid out to wear. Or you hear "I don't have any clean socks!" Why do they always wait until 6:30am to tell us these things? You know you just finished ten loads of laundry and each child had to put away their things. I still believe there is a sock monster.

Quickly filling your coffee mug as full as it can

go, you run out the door only to spill it all over yourself before you get the first sip. You drive the kids to school and pray no one gets sick today.

You then get home and walk through the door of your humble abode and fall over piles of toys and shoes. Thoughts go swirling through your mind as you know just yesterday you spent two hours cleaning the house until it sparkled.

You kick the things out of your way and wade through to the kitchen. Setting your things down, you finally make a new, much needed cup of coffee. Hours pass by like minutes. You rush to pick up what you can. The sink went from empty to full overnight and the smell of the dirty dishes puts you in a bad mood. Time passes, then the clock reads 2:30. It's time to head out for the "pick up."

The kids load into the car like a pack of wild hyenas. Jumping over seats, they are all wanting to fill you in on their day at the same time. No one is paying attention and realizing that others are also talking or that you are staring out the window oblivious to everything. You get home to start homework and dinner. Around 5:30 or so, your spouse comes in from their full day.

You sit down as a family and have dinner. Exhausted and hardly hungry now, you pick at your food while everyone else is eating and happy.

You decide over dinner you need to inform your spouse about little Johnny or Susie's behavior while they eat. After that, you move on to all the frustrations that you encountered that day and then can't seem to understand why, now, your spouse is also in a foul mood.

Dinner ends and its showers and bed times. Finally, the moment you have been waiting for. Quiet. A slight smile crosses your lips as you move ever so slowly to your favorite spot on the couch. You sit down and put your feet up on the couch, take a deep breath, and then it hits you again. That annoying feeling as you look around your house realizing that all your hard work from the day was wasted.

Toys, book bags, papers from school, dirty dishes, socks and stinky shoes all over the house. The feeling of defeat immediately takes over. You feel alone in this battle. You feel like no one else cares or even wants to help.

Well, this may seem like a crazy version of a day in the life of a parent, but at times life just gets overwhelming. Where is your spouse? Why aren't they helping you? Why can't anyone seem to simply pick up what they leave out?

Here's the deal; in our marriages we can let our emotions build up until we are ready to explode! We may go days with frustrations over housekeeping or disciplining the kids. Then, all of a sudden…BAM!

We hit our spouses over the head with it all at once. Sometimes it may come across as nagging or negativity, when all we really want is to be heard and have some help. At some point or another we all have experienced this in some shape or form. How can things get better?

Here are some important things to remember in your marriage:

- It's a team effort. (Some are thinking... But I do it all by myself!)
- Talk to your spouse about your frustrations when you are not so upset. (Some are saying ... I do, but no one listens!)

- If you and your spouse both give one hundred and ten percent in your marriage (whether it be with helping around the house, making dinner, running errands, etc...) you won't feel so alone.

- It starts with you! Do you feel you are constantly giving, but not getting any help? How is your attitude when you are keeping your home? Are you doing it all out of love for your family? Or are you constantly murmuring under your breath as you clean?

- Men and women do not come from the same planets! No really, we are made so uniquely and what you think the other may already know, sometimes they just don't know!

My personal solution: A while back, I decided that enough was enough. I have five kids, was working a full time job, and I am super active in my church and ministries. I'm responsible for getting dinner on the table, keeping the clothes clean, keeping up the house, making sure everyone is healthy, and the list could go on. At some point, you've got to get real with yourself. I've always been harder on myself.

So, sometimes I have dishes in the sink. Some days, my laundry room looks like a war zone. But now, I can remember that I'm not expected to have everything perfect all the time. My husband is such a help when he can be here, but there are days where I don't see him until 10pm I decided to give myself a "break." I do what I can. I ask for help.

Life goes on and there is always something left to do tomorrow. For today, I choose to enjoy more time with my husband and kids.

Thoughts for today:

1. Stop thinking that chores always need to be 50/50. Start thinking in the mindset of 100/100! Talk to your spouse about the things you are struggling with. Be open and reasonable when you are asking for help. Remember, they already have a lot on their plates too! They may feel like they are drowning as well in other areas. Start communicating!

_____

_____

_____

2. How old are your kids? As I've said before, let's begin teaching them responsibility early. Make a list of the biggest things you need help with. Ask your spouse what they would be willing to do. Work together!

_____

_____

_____

3. Take time for yourself. Enjoy your morning coffee for 5 or 10 minutes. Spend some time talking to God about your day and your needs. It amazes me how the Lord can give me such peace despite the day's circumstances. Ask Him today for that peace. He is waiting to hear from you!

Prayer:

Help me, Lord! I feel like a roller coaster that doesn't end! I am tired and I need You! Please help me to remember what is important. Life is not about having a big fancy home or well-dressed kids. It's about Your love and me showing that to others. Please help me refocus on what is important. Help me to take good care of what you have provided us with and help me to ask others for help before I get overwhelmed. Lord, I'm thankful today to even have a home when so many are without. I'm thankful for all of Your provisions for my family. We are so blessed. Please help me to overcome my negativity when it comes to chores and the housework. I know that with You all things are possible and I can survive even on the worst of days. Again, I praise You for all You have done for me today. In Jesus name, Amen

DAY 16 - THE MONEY PIT

Luke 12:22-32 And He said to His disciples, "For this reason I say to you, do not worry about your life, as to what you will eat; nor for your body, as to what you will put on. For life is more than food, and the body more than clothing. Consider the ravens, for they neither sow nor reap; they have no storeroom nor barn, and yet God feeds them; how much more valuable you are than the birds! And which of you by worrying can add a single hour to his life's span? If then you cannot do even a very little thing, why do you worry about other matters? Consider the lilies, how they grow: they neither toil nor spin; but I tell you, not even Solomon in all his glory clothed himself like one of these. But if God so clothes the grass in the field, which is alive today and tomorrow is thrown into the furnace, how much more will He clothe you? You men of little faith! And do not seek what you will eat and what you will drink, and do not keep worrying. For all these things the nations of the world eagerly seek; but your Father knows that you need these things. But seek His kingdom, and these things will be added to you. Do not be afraid, little flock, for your Father has chosen gladly to give you the kingdom.

In the world today, it is not unlikely that many are struggling financially. Whether you are a one or two income house, the struggles are the same. Cost of living has increased dramatically, while our salaries stay the same. You may be caught up in financial hardships or you may have plenty in the bank. One thing that is consistent, no matter what state you are in is that talk of money can be a huge frustration for many couples. I've been financially stable in my own life where I didn't have to worry about emergencies or the unexpected. I've also had the bank account drained to the end. I've lived through the frustration of not knowing how we will pay our bills. It's an extremely scary place to be.

However, if you have faith in the Lord, you know one way or another it will work out in the end. We have had good times and bad. We've had many job changes along with job loss. We made it through two years of unemployment. This was only preparation for what God was about to do.

Sometimes you take your financial security for granted. I believe God was reminding us that we live by faith in Him and not of ourselves.

So many people fight over money. It is the root cause of many disagreements. One might say, "my spouse spends way too much!" While another may say, "my spouse won't let me spend anything!" Either way, you get my point. How can you work together towards the same goal of less debt and more security?

First of all, you need to get on the same wavelength. Life is not about all the "stuff" we want or accumulate. I've been in so many houses where you can't even move around because every spot is cluttered with more junk. Doesn't the Bible talk about storing treasures in heaven and not here on earth?

Am I saying that you can't get that new outfit or buy that boat you have been saving for? No way! I'm all about setting goals and treating yourself every once in a while, but what I am saying is stop wasting what the Lord has blessed you with!

Steve and I began doing the Dave Ramsey study, "Financial Peace University." It's something you do as a couple and I can't tell you how excited this makes me. I desire to live as debt free as possible, but it is all about changing your attitude about spending. I highly recommend looking into this. It's time we put our differences aside and start to work as a team to grow a better future not only for us, but also for the kids.

We need to be teaching our children that you have to work to earn. You have to save up and actually WAIT to buy something you really want. Our world is so revolved around instant gratification that our kids have no clue what they are about to get into as they age. So, let's help them out by setting a good example!

Thoughts for today:

1. Do you find yourself arguing over money frequently? Write down what the exact issue is that upsets you? Is it too much spending or is someone out of work at this time?

_____

_____

_____

_____

_____

2. Now…write down three ways you can "cut back" on spending in your home. You write down your own ways and let your spouse write down theirs. This is not a finger pointing session. Are you eating out every day? Are you buying a coffee every morning?

_____

_____

_____

_____

_____

_____

3. Talk with your spouse about your financial goals. Set a small goal first such as building your savings to $_____ amount or paying off that unwanted bill you get every month.

4. Are you giving back to God?

_____

Did you know this is a huge step of obedience

when you are a follower of Christ? Give your "first fruits" to Him and watch how He will direct your life and help you manage things better.

Prayer:

God, I get so frustrated when we have to talk about money. I just wish the bills would go away and we wouldn't have to worry about everything month to month. It gets so overwhelming some days! I know Lord, that You tell us not to worry about what we have here on this earth, but help me refocus. I want to be a giver not a hoarder. I want to be smart with what You have given us. Please help us to be able to communicate better about these important issues. Help us to be obedient and give to You. Help us to remember that everything we have is because of YOU and it is not our own. Thank you for being our Provider in times of need! I praise You today for our marriage and I pray You will help us grow closer together through this. In Your name we pray, Amen!

DAY 17 - MONEY: FRIEND OR FOE

Proverbs 22:7 The rich rule over the poor, and the borrower is servant to the lender.

Adrian Rogers once said: "It's about time we stopped buying things we don't need with money we don't have to impress people we don't like."

Have you ever really read the verse above and understood its meaning? It says we are "servants to the lender." So we are enslaved to those who we owe money to! Wow! That's a new way to think about debt!

As I said before, Steve and I are going through Dave Ramsey's study. It's awesome and I recommend it to everyone no matter what financial state you are in. We want to have security and a healthy financial future for our family. We want to live as comfortable as possible. It's scary to think of our children eventually needing five cars, five sets of tuition for college, five weddings, etc...

In many blended families, there may be child support payments, alimony, or other costs that affect your home budget. Depending on if you are on the giving or receiving end of that it could help or hurt. So what can you do to help build a healthy financial future for your family?

Here are some great tips that we've enforced in our own marriage. The following tips have come from parents, friends, and financial counselors:

1. Don't spend more than what you earn. This is a very simple concept. If you don't have the money to buy something, don't buy it! Yes, we all have emergencies. The tire may go flat, someone may need an ER visit, the car may need to be fixed, or you may have some other unexpected costs. But overall, there are wants and then there are needs. It just takes a little prioritizing, but you can do this!

2. Don't make large purchases on a whim. Whenever we have to buy a car or something that's expensive, we prayerfully consider it first. We look into all other options and pray for God's guidance. You know that as soon as your drive onto a car lot you will be swarmed with eager salesman wanting you to buy on the spot.

Most of the time, you can tell them what price range you are looking at, but be assured they will show you options outside of what you know you can afford. Don't get caught up in all the excitement of the moment. I always chuckle a little when we find what we like and turn to the salesman and say, "Well, this is the one we want, but we are going to go home now and pray about it and we will let you know."

You may wake up satisfied the next day with your decision or you may feel unrest about it. Either way, it is always good to stop and think before deciding.

3. Don't drive through fast food restaurants just because it is convenient. Learn to cook at home more often. My kids enjoy cooking. Not only are we saving money by eating at home, but they are learning important skills for their future. This will also give you much needed family time.

4. Don't buy expensive items without consulting each other first. This is just a common courtesy to your spouse. Usually there is one who is the budgeter and one who is the spender. I want to ensure that Steve and I are in agreement before either one of us goes for a big ticket item.

You may want to set a limit. For example, we won't purchase anything over $200 without consulting the other. This will save you from many disagreements related to money.

I heard recently that the number one cause for divorce today is fighting over money! Really?! I can think of much worse, but MONEY????!!!!! I was shocked to think that this could be the demise of so many marriages, but it is true.

If you are a couple that has frequent fights over money, it's time to stop. Not including the fact that a lot of us are in second marriages which also have a very high failure rate. I wouldn't wish divorce on anyone! It's a terrible thing to have to go through. So, protect your relationships today and start communicating about this important subject.

Thoughts for today:

1. If you don't have one already, write a budget. If you don't know how, or don't know where to start email me at brokentoblendeministries@gmail.com and I will be happy to show you how to get started.

If you already have a budget, are you actively using it? When was the last time you looked at all your debits, checks, and charges and compared them to your budget?

---

2. Discuss the family budget with your spouse. Once you both agree with what is written, then share it with your family. Teach your kids what it means to work for what you have. Teach them the importance of treating your home and belongings with   care.

3. Set a few goals financially. For example, do you want to have $_____ in savings in the next four months or is there some debt you would like paid off sooner? Start working towards your goals together.

Prayer:

Lord, I don't want to end up in another failed marriage. I want to love and respect my spouse just as I would like to be treated. I know this means I need to work diligently in every area of my marriage including finances. Please help me to communicate with my spouse about any financial decisions I am not comfortable with or concerns I might have. I know, Lord, that all we have is not because of us; it's because of You! I want to be responsible with what you have given us. Please lead us today and help us grow closer together as we discuss the subject of money. Thank you for all you've blessed us with. In Your name we pray, Amen!

DAY 18 - LIFE AS A SOAP OPERA

2 Corinthians 12:9-10 But he said to me, "My grace is sufficient for you, for my power is made perfect in weakness." Therefore I will boast all the more gladly about my weaknesses, so that Christ's power may rest on me. That is why, for Christ's sake, I delight in weaknesses, in insults, in hardships, in persecutions, in difficulties. For when I am weak, then I am strong.

There have been many times in my life when I have felt like I'm living a real life soap opera. Nope, I've never actually watched one, but I've seen enough previews to get the point. DRAMA!

Do you ever ask yourself why so many people are interested in those shows? I do. I just didn't get it really until my life started to feel like one. I noticed that no one really paid much attention to me or my life until it took a nasty twist.

Of course, I had plenty of people loving and

supporting me throughout my life, but others came out of the woodwork when I went through my divorce. For those of you who have been through this, you understand. It's the people who decide that they have a "need to know" about details of your personal life.

When you are in the middle of your storm, you are not always clear headed. It's hard to be discerning of who to talk to and who not to talk to. Some people portray themselves as caring, but once you pour your heart and soul out, it comes back to bite you. Details of your life are on display for all to see.

I grew up a pastor's daughter; the baby girl to be exact. My dad was the pastor at the same church for forty years. It was, and still is, my home. I call many my friends and family there. That is where I met my first husband.

My parents had a rule that we date someone within our church family. This was their way of teaching us to find a partner who shared the same beliefs. It doesn't always work that way in some places. Where I live now, I can't imagine a parent saying that. The churches are too small and there aren't enough young people involved these days.

Anyhow, we dated in the public eye. I think, when so many people feel like your family, they also feel the need to have a say in "approving" the one you are to marry. This was fine with me. I knew that people were almost just as protective as my own parents.

As I dated, there were red flags that I noticed. I remember talking to my dad about them. Most of them were about how I envisioned my husband to be and, when things didn't match up I wasn't quite sure how to react. But, I continued on as if nothing was wrong.

A few years later, we married. (This is not going to be a bash session for my ex. I don't believe in that and am not writing this to hurt anyone.) After a few months of marriage, some bad habits began to show. These were not things that I knew about or they would have been "deal breakers."

Unfortunately, there was nothing I could do about it, either. I was young and naive and thought that things would just get better on their own. These times would come and go, but, when they came, it would get worse with each episode.

I remember crying so many times because that was all I knew to do. I would cry out to God and ask Him why I was dealing with this situation. Still, no answer came. Years passed and we had Hailey. When Hailey was two, we decided to move to Tennessee for a new job he got.

Leaving my home and my church were some of the hardest things in my life still today. I loved Tennessee, but shortly after moving I realized life had changed. I was eight months pregnant with Avery and felt very lonely. I had no friends, no family nearby, and no church to call my own. We church hopped (which is so uncomfortable for me) until we found a place to stay.

Within a matter of a year, I came to a place where I felt like I was drowning. Our marriage had hit rock bottom and I felt the worst betrayal possible. There I was, twenty-six, with two very young girls, and making the decision to start a new life.

Anger, pain, and bitterness engulfed every bit of my being. I felt numb. I had no tears left to cry. My future was gone. I couldn't think past a day or two without feeling a sense of utter defeat. But, in the midst of my worst fear coming true, I was not alone.

My God was with me. He held my hand. He picked me up and carried me when I couldn't walk any farther.

You may be asking, "Why did she get into all this?" Or maybe you're thinking "what's the point?" The point is....... YOU ARE NOT ALONE!!!! I don't care if you are single, happily married, separated, divorced, widowed, or whatever the case may be. Everyone at some point in their life feels like they are in a complete state of disrepair. That their life was all a complete lie or that you will never know where to even start picking up the pieces!

YOU DON'T HAVE TO! God is there and will heal the broken. He will carry the weak. He will give you the strength to make it through life's struggles! I am living proof!

I hate to watch others hurt and go through the same pains. I can almost relive the exact pain with them and it brings back painful memories. But, it is healing.

I pray every day that God uses my testimony to help others. I am stronger today because of what I have come through. I am a work in progress and He's not finished with me yet! PRAISE GOD!!!

Thoughts for today:

1. Do you have a hard time talking about your past? _____

I have found that the more I share with others; the more comfortable I become. God wants to use our stories. You were not an accident; nor was your life!

2. What is the primary topic of your story?
_____
Does your story involve divorce, death, drugs, alcohol, adultery, or abuse? Maybe it's something else. Think of all the people you could encourage with your life!

3. What is holding you back from being transparent with others? Do you feel people will judge you? Do you not want to pull out all your "dirty little secrets?"

_____
_____
_____
_____

Here's the deal! God has a great purpose for your life. Until you decide to start living your life for Him and not for your own well-being, you will never know how it feels to truly be trusting in God. To have complete dependence on Him is one of the bases of our faith. Will you let Him use you today?

Prayer:

God, it's so painful to relive my past. I wish I could erase all the battle scars from my mind and pretend it never happened, but that would be a lie. I haven't come this far in vain. I want to be used by you, Lord, for whatever purpose You may have for me. I'm scared and I'm vulnerable to what others may think, however, I am Your creation. You know me best! I pray today, God, that you will fight this battle in my heart with me. I know that, with You, I can share with others and help someone today. Please help me to be bold! Thank you for Your forgiveness and Your mercy. In Jesus name, Amen!

DAY 19 - A FEAR OF THE FUTURE

Matthew 6:34 Therefore do not worry about tomorrow, for tomorrow will worry about itself. Each day has enough trouble of its own.

Fear is real. It can be crippling. It can literally stop you from moving forward in your life.

When I became a single mom, I entered one of the scariest portions of my life... having to leave my kids. I am the primary custodial parent for the girls, but they would still visit their dad every other weekend. We lived in two different states. I remember the fear that engulfed me when I had to drop them off that first time. I had NEVER been without the girls overnight. I didn't fear them being with their dad, I feared them being without me. What if they got sick? What if they were in an accident?

For months, I would cry after dropping them off. Not in front of them, but as I watched the car pull away, my heart would break. I knew what they would be exposed to when they left and I had no control of the situation. It killed me to have them go to a house where a stranger would be taking my place. They were too young to talk to me about it since they were only one and three. So, unless someone told me what was going on, I was not privy to the information.

Then came the fear of the future. I started to think about if something happened to me. Who would raise the girls? If they lived with their dad, would they be able to see my family? I can't tell you the countless thoughts that raced through my mind.

Then the thoughts turned to nightmares. I would wake up in the night crying, fearful that something terrible would happen while they were gone. I was so caught up in all of my emotional distress that it took me a while to remember that God had complete control and He had his hand on the girls.

It is so easy to get wrapped up in situations and forget that we were never in control in the first place! As the kids have gotten older, my nerves have learned to relax. I can't say that I don't get concerned when they are gone, but I've learned to be dependent upon my Heavenly Father rather than myself.

If you have to leave your kids from time to time, don't spend the entire weekend worrying. God tells us to "cast all our cares upon Him!" Some days you might get to talk with them and others pass when you have called five times and no one answers.

Instead of being overwhelmed with worry or concern, let's refocus. Maybe this can be a time for you to spend focusing on your relationship with the Lord.

For me, it's a time to regroup. Sometimes I jump into a project at home or jump into the kid's stuff and just clean out. Other times, Steve and I may get out for a much needed date or just have extra time to be together.

Whatever it may be, don't let fear take your every bit of energy. I could choose to stay in bed and sulk all weekend, or I can choose to be motivated. I've learned that in whatever situation, I'm going to choose to be happy and content.

I'm thankful for the time that I am given with the kids. Life could be worse. Others may have a much more difficult situation than you! It's time to praise God for what He has blessed you with.

Thoughts for today:

1. Do you find yourself fearful when your kids are gone? Write down your biggest fears or concerns.

---

2. Now, which of those do you have control over? NONE! You can't control what happens to your children just like you cannot control what happens to you! I want you to turn each of these fears over

to God. You may have to do this daily. You may only have to do this when they leave, but either way it's time to hand it over. You've been carrying this burden long enough.

3. What kind of relationship do you have with your ex? Are you able to communicate without arguing?

_____

Can you work together to plan out trips or schedules? _____

It's time to start fresh. If you aren't to this place yet; you won't get peace until you do. Stop pointing fingers! It starts with you today! If you want to have a healthy relationship with your ex and have your children see how it can work despite your past, just do it! It is possible! Check yourself and your attitude!

Prayer:

Lord, you know my deepest fear as a parent. I never want anything bad to happen to my kids, but I also know I can't control this. I pray today that You will give me a peace that I know only comes from You!! I give you my children and I give you my fears. Please help me to work hard at showing your love to everyone - even my ex! I want my kids to see Your love pour out of me and that all things are possible with You! Please help me when they are gone. Help me to know You are watching over them. Lord, I want to live a happy life and I know that starts with joy from You. I praise You for the time you have given me with my children. May I not take this time for granted. In Jesus name, Amen!

DAY 20 - PRAYING PARENTS

James 5:16 Confess your faults one to another, and pray one for another, that ye may be healed. The effectual fervent prayer of a righteous man availeth much.

I'm not a perfect parent and I'm definitely nowhere near a perfect person. I am very human with, unfortunately, daily failures of my own. Parenting is full of trials and errors.

I always joke with the oldest that he is the "guinea pig," when in fact he truly is! We learn by doing. We have been taught certain aspects of parenting by how we were raised and the rest we figure out as we go. We are faced with difficult decisions on a daily basis and our children are dependent on us for a time to make important choices for them.

As they grow, we have to learn to trust them to make choices on their own. If we continue to make our kids decisions for them as they age, we aren't teaching them how to be independent thinkers.

This is such a hard thing for me to handle sometimes. I would love to just tell them what to do and call it a day, but it's not that easy. I find myself giving them permission to choose wisely, then end up backtracking and worrying about what they will do.

Sometimes being a parent also means we have to ask our children to forgive us. It's a humbling experience when you have to tell your child your behavior was wrong.

However, if you don't show your kids this side, you are teaching them that they don't have to say "I'm sorry" or ask forgiveness when needed. Parents mess up! Kids make mistakes! It's normal! Let's teach them the right way to handle it!

Prayer is an amazing tool that God has given us. We can choose to use it or abuse it. Coming to God in prayer doesn't mean we are only to come to Him with wants or needs. We need to be consistently talking with Him about the good and the bad.

Have you ever noticed when you are going through a difficult time you tend to pray more? Why do we use God like this? Why do we simply ignore Him until we "decide" that we need Him right then at that moment?

I've been guilty about this as well. I know that when my life was not all "rainbows and sunshine" I found myself crying out to God more often. Now, I have come to realize that I need to have that daily time with Him. I may be driving, working, cooking, or having my quiet time when I call on Him. I talk to Him throughout my day and not just over meals or at bedtime. I can find a peace in Him and I have more of a dependency on my God when I share more of my life with Him.

We can't depend on our own knowledge and direction to raise our children. If we want them to grow up knowing how mighty God is, we need to show them by our own actions and our own spiritual life.

Thoughts for today:

1. Do you pray with your family? Is it only during meals or at bedtime? Let's break this tradition and start teaching them to call on the Lord throughout the day.

---

2. Do you find yourself praying only when you are in a mess? It is so easy to do. Sometimes people feel awkward about praying because they just don't know how to do it right. Well, there is no right or wrong way to talk with God. He wants you to call on Him! Just start by thanking Him for the blessings in your life. Talk to Him about your struggles and your desires. He is calling you today to spend more time with Him!

3. Start keeping a prayer journal for your kids. Write each child's name down and specifics for

each that you want to pray about. Sometimes it is their character traits or behavior you pray for. Maybe they don't know the Lord yet! An awesome thing we can do as parents is to pray that one day they would come to know God! Take time daily and cover your kids in prayer.

Prayer:

Dear Lord, I come to you today wanting to have a more intimate relationship with you. I don't want you waiting for me to speak with you. I want to continuously talk with you throughout my day. Help me to learn how to have a stronger prayer life. Help me and my spouse to learn how to pray together without it feeling awkward. Help me to realize the importance of covering the children in prayer daily. I pray for my kids today. I pray that You will help me be the parent I need to be. Help them to see my walk with you as a help, and not a hindrance, to their spiritual life. Help them to learn to be dependent upon you, Lord! Thank you for guiding me through this life as a parent. Amen!

DAY 21 - THE GUILT TRIP

Psalm 38:4 For my iniquities are gone over my head; as a heavy burden they weigh too much for me.

Psalm 23:1-3 The Lord is my shepherd, I shall not want. He makes me lie down in green pastures; He leads me beside quiet waters. He restores my soul; He guides me in the paths of righteousness For His name's sake.

The girls were asleep, yet I sat on my bed unable to rest. It was late. It had been a full day of running around to work, daycare, and now to my parent's house where I had recently moved into. My heart was so heavy and my spirit so worn.

I had been so strong, but at this moment I didn't know how long I could keep up the show. I was dying inside. I didn't know what the future held and I felt so incredibly hurt.

Despite my confidence in the decision I had made, I felt a sense of guilt for my children. The thought of divorce had never crossed my mind. I was in my marriage for life! I took my vows seriously!

How did this all happen? I remember the pain as if it was today. I can feel the emotions boil inside of me in an instant when I think back to this time. Have I completely ruined my kids' lives? How will I give them what they need on my own? I can't live with my parents forever!

I cried out to the Lord! No words; just tears. I laid there in my bed praying for direction and for the strength to endure the storm.

Have you ever been there? Are you there now? The pain and fear are so traumatic at times that it is hard to look past it. When you are caught up in the whirlwind, you just can't seem to get see through it.

During this time in my life, my dad was my rock. My family was there for me at the lowest point in my life. I remember my dad would call me at work and take me out to lunch for some time alone. He allowed me to talk through my hurts and he would give me scripture to help me along. He held my hand through this emotional journey and was there when I couldn't stand going to court alone.

I remember one day as he sat studying for his sermon in the hall of the courts while I was handling my case. I would come out in tears and my dad would help pick up the pieces.

If my earthly father was there for me at such a time, imagine how God was there with me! God is there for you also!

Did you read the verses above? It says that "he restores my soul!" God is love! God is forgiveness! God is all merciful and powerful! He will take that guilt and that pain from you! My dad is an amazing man of God, but my God is so much more!

If you are still struggling with your past today, allow God to take this guilt and pain. He's been trying, but you have been clinging to it! Why suffer through this hurt any longer?

I'm so amazed at His love for us! HE DIED FOR YOU! How could you show love any stronger than what Jesus did on that cross? Get rid of the grief, the grudge, the anger, and the guilt! Be free in Him today! All things are possible with God!

Thoughts for today:

1. What are you feeling guilty about?

_____

_____

How long have you been in the bonds of your pain and grief?

_____

2. Scripture memorization is healing. Did you know that when you are going through a tough time, God can remind you of His words? Try to memorize the 23rd Psalm. It will be a challenge,

but so worth it!

3. God wants you to lead a full, happy life! He can free us from the bondage of sin or shame! Do you have a personal relationship with Him? If you don't, please contact me and I will show you how you can have this amazing life with God! If you do know Him, can others see your joy in Him? It's time to let go and let God direct you today! Will you join me?

Prayer:

Lord, You know my very core! You know the pains and guilt I have felt over my life. Sometimes I simply don't know how to get through it. I know Satan loves to remind me of my past faults, but with You, Lord, I know I can see the light in the darkness. I want to use my past experiences as a time for growth and not as a crutch. God, help me today to take off my chains that are weighing me down. Use me and use my life as a living testimony! I'm ready to start fresh and move on. Create in me a clean heart, oh God, and renew a right spirit within me! Amen!

DAY 22 - BATTLING THE DEVIL

Ephesians 6:10-13 KJV
Finally, my brethren, be strong in the Lord, and in the power of his might. Put on the whole armor of God that ye may be able to stand against the wiles of the devil. For we wrestle not against flesh and blood, but against principalities, against powers, against the rulers of the darkness of this world, against spiritual wickedness in high places. Wherefore take unto you the whole armor of God that ye may be able to withstand in the evil day, and having done all, to stand.

I love it when days go by smoothly. Although, we know that it is only for a time. Today, I was on a Jesus high. It was the end of the week and I was cruising through my day.

Then, out of nowhere the devil uses someone to throw me off track. Do you ever wonder if people just hate their jobs or their lives so much that they are out to destroy you also? Well, that's what happened to me.

I just happened to call the wrong person at the wrong time. I think they were looking for someone to pounce on. Little did I know that after a friendly "hello" there would be a five minute long conversation that would leave me in disgust.

As I stood there in silence, after hanging up my phone, I had so many thoughts. The first one that came to my mind was "bring it on Satan!" I knew that this was of the devil.

My day was going well and I knew that my husband was in deep prayer mode for the last twenty-four hours. I usually expect issues to arise during times of fasting. I cried out to God. I quoted scripture and told Satan that he had no authority over my life.

At any time that could be us! Our daily lives are full of decisions, especially related to our attitude and outlook on life. I have to make a decision every day to live my life as a reflection of Christ.

I want others to look at me and say "Hey! What's different about her?" I want people to ask me why I am happy. I want to be a witness without even using words!

You never know when someone has had a terrible time with life. They could be on the brink of a making a terrible decision and I don't want to be that person to push them over the edge. It's a challenge for sure, but God knows that we are capable of using our words wisely.

Did you read the scripture above? The children of God are in a constant fight with the devil. He wants to devour us and ruin us. We need to clothe ourselves in God's armor.

This life is a battle of Good versus Evil. God's people against the devil and his followers. Who said being a follower of Christ was easy? Not me!

However, God gave us the armor to be our tools. Go ahead and read all of Ephesians 6 today. Look down the list of each individual piece He gives us to protect us.

I always say that I know God won't give me more than I can handle. It's such an easy thing to say, but to live it is the hard part. Clothe yourself today in His armor! For the battle has only just begun!

Thoughts for today:

1. Do you face spiritual warfare with Satan? Is he constantly trying to disrupt your life? Call out to God. Tell Satan to "get lost!"

2. Don't let Satan get the best of your life and deplete your emotions and energy. That's his goal! Instead, ask God to give you the strength to battle him. Ask God for His protection over you and your family. Cover your family in prayer and keep yourself in check.

3. Don't allow Satan to use you as his tool to discourage others. Let your life be a light in the darkness. Show God's love to others by your words and actions. Let's keep each other accountable with this. We don't want to turn people away from the Lord, but rather draw them

closer to Him!

Prayer:

God, You know the day I've had. I've had the hardest time remaining focused on You due to Satan attacking me any way possible. I know that You give me the strength to endure these tests, but help me to be an example with how I handle my emotions and words. Let my life reflect Your love and mercy. Help me to have great self control. I love you, God, and I know You are right here with me through it all! Thank you for your steadfast love! Amen!

DAY 23 - FINDING YOUR PLACE

Proverbs 2:6 For the Lord gives wisdom; from His mouth come knowledge and understanding.

Proverbs 9:10 The fear of the Lord is the beginning of wisdom and the knowledge of the Holy One is understanding.

Blending into a new family with more children can be a big undertaking. I always thought I would have my two girls, the house with the white picket fence, and a simple life to raise them in. Well, obviously that dream wasn't the blueprint for my life.

When Steve and I decided to merge our families into one, little did we know how difficult that would be at times. It wasn't like we could make decisions on our own as if they were "our" children only. We had to consider others. This was not always easy.

There were "marked" territories with certain decisions, even as simple as taking a child for a haircut or to the doctor when they were sick. Everything, and I mean everything, had to pass a point of approval.

I am not the type that functions well in this type of surrounding. If a child is sick, I will take them to the doctor. If someone's hair is unruly, we go for a trim.

Well, blended families have much more to deal with when making simple decisions. Sometimes, the little things that you do to show love or support to the children will promote backlash after the fact. Then there are other times, like we've talked about before, when you are reminded that you are not "the parent."

Oh glorious day! I think that is one thing that can get under my skin quicker than a bee gets to a honeysuckle! You know, when you are pouring your time and energy out only to be slapped in the face with a comment like that.

Believe me, it doesn't happen often. Thanks to some talks I've had with the kids and how that makes others feel; they are on the same wavelength as me now. But, this has been a "sore spot" in the past.

So what do you do? Where is your place in the family? How can you work through all these frustrations that simply will NOT go away!?!

The verse above says a lot about this. God is wisdom, knowledge, AND understanding. What? Say that again?! God is understanding!

I get so caught up trying to make it work myself and trying to figure out other people's reasons for their actions when in fact, it really doesn't matter. There is no point sometimes trying to "fix" things that only God can fix.

I find myself asking God for wisdom all the time. It could be a petty reason or something I feel is a big deal. But you know what? God thinks my life is important.

He made me. He knows how I think and how I respond. He formed my brain and knows what it will take for me to understand the situation I am in. I can't do this alone. My husband and I can't depend solely on each other to run our family smoothly. We can't do it!

Only with God's help can we make the right decisions and keep from reacting the way we would really like to! It's a daily surrender. It's not easy. When we get over one hump; we get smacked in the face with something else. It's life. God didn't intend for it to be like this.

However, instead of dwelling on how we got here; let's move forward and make it the best it can be! I can learn to adapt with God by my side. It's not the end of the world when I can't do what I want to do. It's time to put selfishness aside and start to look at things through the eyes of others. I get way too tired trying to run on the hamster wheel that goes nowhere.

Instead, from now on, I will run the race with God and let Him guide my moves. My "place" is in Him alone. Yes, I'm a mom, step-mom, and wife, but that's not who I am in Christ. I am a child of the King! Think about finding your place IN HIM today!

Thoughts for the day:

1. Do you hear "you can do this, but not that" way too much?! As long as it's not affecting the kids, then it's time we move away from this frustration. Let's stop getting caught up in the he said/she said and focus on who Christ wants us to be and how He wants us to react.

2. If you are a believer in Him, He is with you. So, next time we get in a "sticky" situation with another parent, remember He is right there listening to your every word. If we can keep ourselves in check, we have nothing to worry about. If we fly off the handle and react, we are only feeding into the devil. He is rejoicing when we lose control.

3. Your place in your family is so important. You are a leader. You are guiding your kid's footsteps. Which way are you leading them? I want to lead my kids into a world where they make godly decisions and not care what the world thinks. However, that starts with my spouse and I. If we don't show them how to find wisdom, knowledge, and understanding through Christ and His scriptures, where will they learn this?

Prayer:

Dear Lord, I am done trying to find my place in this world. I need to focus on You first and only then will I gain the knowledge and wisdom I need to raise my family. Please help me to take the "me me me" out of it and replace it with You and Your scriptures. You give us these words for a reason and I want to use them as my parenting manual. Help me to disregard the little things that get under my skin and focus on the big picture. Help my kids to see that we are depending on You through this life; not on our own understanding. We love you Lord and are ready to move forward! Amen!

DAY 24 - THE NOT-SO-HALLMARK HOLIDAYS

Proverbs 31:25-27 Strength and dignity are her clothing and she smiles at the future. She opens her mouth in wisdom, And the teaching of kindness is on her tongue. She looks well to the ways of her household, And does not eat the bread of idleness.

Lamentations 3:22-24 The Lord's loving kindnesses indeed never cease, For His compassions never fail. They are new every morning; Great is Your faithfulness. "The Lord is my portion," says my soul, "Therefore I have hope in Him."

Have you ever wanted to make up your own version of a song? Well, I did, with my twisted sense of humor. So, sing this with me...

(Sing this song with the Jingle Bells tune)
Dashing through the snow
In a big ole' SUV
Around the mountains we go
Wishing it wasn't me

The kids are packed in tight
Their bags fill up the car
Days or weeks they come and go
And we know what's in store.....

Oh..... kids go here
Kids go there
Isn't that such fun
You think the weeks just started out
But it's only just begun oh.......

Ok! Yes, I know I am a little crazy, but sometimes you just have to laugh a little at life. When families are blended, it makes life difficult during the holidays. What should be fun and memorable, sometimes turns out to be dreaded.

Think about it! What happens on Mother's Day, Father's Day, Thanksgiving, and Christmas? It's time for families to come together to celebrate Jesus, life, each other, and God's blessings. However, this all changes when you're a step-parent or have a blended family.

Being a step-mom, I don't expect a "Happy Mother's Day" welcome or card from my step-kids. After all, they have their own mom. If I get one, it's a pleasant surprise. I don't go into it with expectations.

What I do like is when my husband reminds me of how far we've come as a family. He thanks me for helping raise his kids and tells me how special and important I am to him. I believe once I found my place in our family and understood how to better adjust during these times, it made my life a little less complicated.

Father's Day is the same way. Steve doesn't go in with expectations either. It's a little different for us in this way because the two younger girls have called Steve "Dad" from the start. They were very young and it came naturally, so I didn't interfere.

The older two children weren't as young. They feel more comfortable calling me by my first name, which actually feels more comfortable to me as well.

So, what about Christmas, Thanksgiving, and Easter? Honestly, it's not easy. I remember when I was a kid. We would spend entire days if not a week at my grandparent's home in Arkansas. My parents didn't have to drag us from one home to the next and break up our fun.

Not so with our blended bunch. We have to plan ahead and hope no one else changes the plans as the time gets closer. Think about this… four parents and seven grandparents and that doesn't include the great-grandparents we visit!

As much as I would love to say that I enjoy holidays, sometimes I just don't. By the end of Christmas break, Steve and I find ourselves exhausted physically and sometimes emotionally.

As the kids age, it does get a little easier. In the next few years, some of the kids will be driving themselves from one house to the other. I hate to say it, but we are really excited about that! I think when the children are young, we want to give them those special memories that we had as kids. But, at times, it's hard to see past the frustrations.

So, how do you survive the "not-so-Hallmark holidays?" First of all, don't set yourself up for disappointment. Don't make unachievable expectations. Instead, why not come up with some ideas of your own to start your very own traditions?

This is a way that I like to make memories with my family. For example, we like to make homemade ornaments, crafts, and gingerbread men every year around Christmastime. I can do all of these things BEFORE they go here, there, and everywhere!

Secondly, make an alternating schedule so every other year you will have the same routine with where the kids will be. This will take away the stress of having to communicate over and over again about the same holidays.

In addition, be considerate of all parties involved. Sometimes, we may just need to step back and look at things from a different angle. With time and patience, it's very possible to make things work for you and your family. Things don't always go as we planned, but at least we have time together!

I'm thankful for every day that God gives me with my family! If we can view it as quality versus quantity, you can still maintain great memories with each year that passes.

Thoughts for today:

1. What is your most stressful or frustrating holiday? Why?

_____

_____

_____

_____

_____

2. How can you make it more enjoyable for your entire family? Sometimes this means staggering family visits each year instead of always trying to be everywhere all of the time. Plan ahead! Who says you can't celebrate before the kids go or after they return. I've found myself planning it this way. I can still celebrate with family even if the kids are not present. You may have to postpone your plans for a time you can really sit back and enjoy it more.

_____

_____

_____

_____

_____

3. Be reminded today of the hope God gives us. Life will not always be as complicated as it can be in blended families with young kids. Eventually, our kids will grow up and have lives and schedules of their own. Our holiday hopping will be a distant memory. But you know what I believe? I believe that if we try to make it work to the best of our abilities and sit back and enjoy the time we

have, THEN...... one magical day our children will say to us "Hey! Do you remember that Christmas when....." They will begin to recall those special times you did have together and it will be worth the efforts you put forth.

Prayer:

Dear Lord, I know that life isn't always focused on what I want, but sometimes I just want to have a holiday where I don't feel like we have to try so hard to make it work. I get stressed and out of sorts if things don't go as I had planned. Please help me remember that it's not about all the crazy holiday madness, but holidays are about being thankful for Your amazing blessings on our lives. Thank you, Father, for giving me each day with my family. Thank you for allowing us to make these special memories that will last a lifetime. Amen!

DAY 25 - SBLENDED - A NEW WORD FOR THE DICTIONARY

Matthew 5:16 Let your light shine before men in such a way that they may see your good works, and glorify your Father who is in heaven.

My new word: *Sblended* - (meaning) splendidly blended or a "special" blend.

You're probably wondering why I've come up with my own word now. First a song and now making up words! This girl is crazy!

Well, sometimes when there aren't the right words to describe what we have, we just improvise. I know we've talked a lot about the frustrations that blended families can face, but now let's talk about the joys.

Did you know that your family is so special to God? Did you know that He wants only the best for you? God has brought your family together for a purpose.

He blended your gang together and wants to see your family grow together in love. The parents are the key to seeing this through. We are the examples.

Did you read the verse above? "Let your light shine before men..." Lead by example. If we want to have a family who loves the Lord, it starts with us. Here are a few starter tips:
- Love, respect, and honor your spouse.
- Be uplifting to them and don't tear them down.
- Show affection in front of the kids.
- Pray together and have a time for family devotions.
- Be transparent with your kids. Let them know we all make mistakes.
- Be honest! If kids see their parents lying, they will follow in those footsteps.
- Be accountable to your spouse.
- Show acts of love to each child. Each child is different and requires a different approach.
- Give your family structure and guidance by having a routine that they can follow.

I want people to know that no matter how my family came together or why, we survived the test! We have made it work!

For those who don't know us, we pass for your typical "non-blended" family! Not that it's important, but that's my desire for my kids. I want them to love each other with that sibling type of love. You can't force that. If it comes; it comes. If they don't "click" like that; then you just continue to pray. Either way, we can be close-knit.

You know what I just love now? After almost seven years of being "Sblended," my step-kids make sure that they hug and kiss me goodnight. When they leave for school, I get a "love you, Sam!" I don't ask for it. I don't force it. But, now after the years of hard work I'm seeing a payoff!

The other night, the oldest decided to go to bed early. He was exhausted after a long day of sports and school. He got up from where we were sitting and his step-sister said "I love you, Terek!" He turned and told each of the kids he loved them back. I could see a huge smile on Hailey's face as he walked away.

She waited for him to leave the room and said "Mom! That was the first time he's told me he loves me!" Her face said it all! That was "her" brother too! It didn't matter who his Mom or Dad was. She considers him her own flesh and blood.

Praise God for His continued blessings over our family. With Him surrounding every part of our home; we can conquer the challenges. He gives us the strength to endure the hardships and the joy to celebrate the achievements. We give God the glory!

Thoughts for today:

1. Are you following "The Light" or are you still stuck in the darkness with your family? God wants only the best for you and your gang. Allow yourself to be used by Him and for His glory!

2. Are you putting in time to work on your family life? Or are you giving everything or everyone else your time and energy. If you want this to work, it takes consistency and perseverance. Get in the Bible! See all that God says about godly living and raising a family. I don't care how many kids you have or how many marriages you have had. It's time to put the past behind you and start moving FORWARD! You can do this with God's help!

3. What are 2 goals you would like to make for your family? Make them realistic. For example: 1. Spend more quality time together (no tv, no cell phones, but lots of fun). 2. Cut down on the bickering or fighting that plagues your home.

_____

_____

_____

Now, what are some interventions you can do to promote these goals? List 2 things per goal that you are going to do to promote a healthier life at home for you and your family. Now, cover this in prayer daily and watch God work!

_____

_____

_____

_____

Prayer:

Lord, I'm thankful today for Your amazing plan. I may not know what it involves, but I know it's much bigger than I could ever imagine! I want my family to portray your goodness and mercy You have bestowed upon us. I want to be that light that you talk about in Matthew. Please guide us and let my spouse and I work together to bring our family closer. I thank You in advance for what You are about to do in our lives. Thank you for making us SBLENDED! Amen!

DAY 26 - CONTROL FREAK

James 4:6-8 But He gives a greater grace. Therefore it says, "God is opposed to the proud, but gives grace to the humble." Submit therefore to God. Resist the devil and he will flee from you. Draw near to God and He will draw near to you. Cleanse your hands, you sinners; and purify your hearts, you double-minded.

Psalm 61:1-4 Hear my cry, O God; Give heed to my prayer. From the end of the earth I call to You when my heart is faint; Lead me to the rock that is higher than I. For You have been a refuge for me, A tower of strength against the enemy. Let me dwell in Your tent forever; Let me take refuge in the shelter of Your wings. Selah.

When you, or maybe someone you know, sends their children their other parents, there may be "questionable situations" in the other homes that raise concerns. These situations could involve drugs, alcohol, or random people spending the night. Unfortunately, the courts today will not tell your ex to stop risky behavior, even when children are present. I have many friends who worry themselves sick over their children while they are away.

Many ask, "Where is God?" or "why would God allow my kids to go to an unsafe home?" These are real questions. Many people feel forsaken by God when there is nothing more that can be done to protect their children. They are left feeling alone and helpless with no sense of security.

I've had many people talk to me about having to send their kids to a home where alcohol is an issue. They worry over the other parent's ability to think clearly and are concerned about potential for drunk driving. Others worry about live-in girlfriends/boyfriends and their influences. Or sometimes, drugs are a problem; yet, without proof nothing can be done about it.

Unfortunately, we cannot control what someone else decides to do with their body. All we can do is pray our children through these situations and prepare them if there was an emergency of some kind. It's such a hard place to be, but God has promised not to give you more than you can handle. You are stronger than you think and, with His help, you can survive this time in your life!

So, where is God when you feel all is forgotten? He is exactly where you left Him! When you decided that God wasn't enough for you and you needed to take matters in your own hands. Or, when something went wrong and you got mad at

God for the negative things in your life. You put Him in the corner and told Him that He was no help to you. You quit going to church because you weren't "getting anything out of it" or maybe you got mad at someone there.

Maybe you have continued to cry out to Him, but you feel He is not listening! Do you feel deserted? God wants to lead us and make us feel secure. But we have to do our part.

Do you have faith in the Lord? This is what faith is all about. It is not about trusting in Christ when everything in your life is fine and dandy. It's about trusting in his mercy and grace whether times are good or bad. It's a lot easier to trust God when life is going as planned, but we easily take our eyes off of Him when we hit the bumps along the way.

Don't you know that we have a free will with our choices we make? Although many of us who are divorced never wanted to be divorced; we are. We made a decision that will affect us and our family life for a long time. Does God punish us because of this? Are we going to live with turmoil our entire life because of a decision in our past?

God is a forgiving God. He has "cast our sins as far as the East is from the West." He has moved forward, but sometimes we are the ones clinging to the past and living as though it is our present. I see so many people trying to live life today while carrying the heavy burdens of their past because they have never given it over to God.

We tend to be "control freaks" each in our own ways. Of course, I would love to know where my kids are at every moment or what kind of living situation they are in. I want to know what kind of people might babysit them or the friend's houses they visit. I'm a protective parent and it's hard to find peace when you have so many unknowns. Did you know that it IS possible to find peace? With me, I have found that when my relationship with God is stronger and I depend on Him more; only then will I have the peace that I need to get through these difficult times.

You see, it really has nothing to do with other people, my children, or their surroundings. Don't you believe that God can do anything? Didn't you know that He wants the best for your family as well?

So, start putting your faith in Him first. You cannot do anything else at this point. God can do it all without our help. So when you feel like there is no hope...... start over with God. Repent over your lack of faith and begin to trust in Him. Cry out to God for help. He is waiting on you today!

Thoughts for today:

1. Have you gone to court over "behavior" issues? Have you tried to stop the other parent from use of alcohol, drugs, live-in partners, or other risky behavior? It's a fight most do not win in court. Our world does not always consider these issues to be as problematic as we do. It's time to fight this battle with the Lord's help. He is bigger than sin. Write down your biggest fears when the kids are away.

_____

_____

_____

2. When did you start to doubt God's control over your family? Have you taken steps away from Him? Are you covering your family in daily prayer? Are you in your Bible or is it still collecting dust on the nightstand? Did you know that when you focus on the Lord instead of yourself that it will be easier to trust Him for the future? So many times we make our kids and ourselves priority instead of God who should be in first place. It's time for a "spiritual 180." We need to change the direction in which we are heading today. Place your focus on His desire for you. Don't tell God how to do His job! He is more capable than we will ever be!

_____

_____

_____

_____

_____

3. Educate your children. Do not teach your kids to "tattle" on their other parents, but you can prepare them for situations they may find themselves in. As the children age, they will be able to communicate any fears or concerns they have. Listen to them. Don't discuss your feelings about their parents. Just hear them out and see what bothers them the most. With you being a listening ear, they will most likely continue to tell you when something happens. If you get upset and go into a "parental fit," then they will

probably not come to you again. Keep the lines of communication wide open.

Prayer:

Lord, I feel out of control so many times. I want to protect my kids wherever they are, but know that I can't. I want to cling to you, Lord, but so many times I am trying to do this on my own. I don't want to be a control freak; I want to be a JESUS FREAK! Lord, help me to find my peace through You. Please give me the scriptures that I need so I can fill my head with Your promises. Protect my children, Lord, and help me to learn to rest in the comfort of Your arms. Thank you for all You have done in our lives and what You have planned for my family! Amen.

DAY 27 - SAY WHAT?!

1 John 4:18-21 There is no fear in love. But perfect love drives out fear, because fear has to do with punishment. The one who fears is not made perfect in love. We love because he first loved us. Whoever claims to love God yet hates a brother or sister is a liar. For whoever does not love their brother and sister, whom they have seen, cannot love God, whom they have not seen. And he has given us this command: Anyone who loves God must also love their brother and sister.

Have you ever heard the following comments?

* Let the child decide what is right or wrong.

* It's ok for little Johnny to watch rated R movies. After all, he's got to learn about the world sometime!

* My 8 year-old is allowed to use "free speech" at my house, even if it includes cursing.

* Little Susie doesn't have to do chores here. I feel like they will have plenty of that when they are older.

* I don't feel the need to call the teacher just because he is getting an "F" at school. School is really not that important to me anyway.

* I'm ok with the kids "testing" things like sex and drugs. They just need to get it out of their system.

This is not a joke people! This is real life and the real world! I've recently received so much feedback from parents and step-parents that just don't know what to do with their ex-spouses behavior towards raising the kids.

Here is an example of what one friend of mine is going through:

"I think the worst part for me is knowing that their mom just doesn't have the same morals that we do. When they leave our house the rules are very different. Since they were the ages of 8/10 they have been exposed to horror movies, rated R movies full of sex and violence and adult tv shows. They have next to no responsibility at their mom's house and she doesn't care about their education. There is no family structure, chores, or positive influence... Let's give an example. At those ages, she found it appropriate to have them start cursing. Can you imagine an eight year old dropping the "f" bomb every day in front of her mother and it being normal? It was very hard for me to have my step kids that I love dearly be in that situation. I wanted to protect them from it all and put them in a different life situation that was going to grow them into the best people they could be. But I was fighting an impossible fight. I don't have control or the ability to make decisions as a parent. The best I could hope for was to be a good influence. What I've realized, is that the kids see me as their parent. They don't see their mom as a parent. They know that they can walk all over her, don't really respect her, but since she plays the victim-- the kids are in a perpetual state of guilt. With me however, they respect me, they ask my advice, they get their chores done, and they try to impress me by talking about what they learned in school and try to make good grades. I think the emotional toll of being a step parent isn't vocalized very well. I know that I've been so upset at their mom's parenting and how it would affect the kids so negatively. I could just scream! I know that the duty I feel to help them is sometimes overwhelming. My parental emotions and fears are just different as a step mom. As a mom, I give my all. I don't just want to raise kids that are ok, I want to raise extraordinary women that know God. I don't want to raise kids that are getting so-so grades and experimenting with sex and drug at 16. I want to raise kids that are going on mission trips and are truly grounded through their relationships with their parents and God. But it's so hard when things are so different in each household. It's so hard when their own mom admits not wanting what's best for them because it's not what's best for her. What I've realized through this struggle is that I'm changing the kids for the better. Every day, every word, every church service, every prayer. They are changing and getting better, so the situation at their mom's house changes too."

Sometimes, we think "did they really just say that?" I'm so confused sometimes as to who is the parent and who is the child. Why would it be "ok" to give your kids permission to try drugs and have sex? Why would you WANT to expose your kids to violence and sex at a young age on the TV?

Where are the boundaries to protect their eyes, ears, and hearts? When did we, as parents, become so lazy that we just didn't care anymore? Wow! It's a wake-up call for sure!

You know, we can't change what the other parents decide to do at their house, but we can strengthen our children when they are with us. We can teach biblical standards and answer the "why" question. Keeping an open line of communication is so important.

I talk with our kids about everything. If they ask about sex, we talk about it. If I hear about someone they know into drugs, we talk about it. Depending on their age, we give more or less details about each topic.

We also discuss wrong choices. We have all made mistakes in our past, but, as a parent, I don't want my kids to have to experience the pains I had if I can teach them about it early. They will grow up making mistakes of their own, but it is up to us to help steer them when they are younger. My friend said it right. All she can do is be there for her step-kids and give them the positive role model they need.

Prayer can change lives! Get on your knees and pray for that parent who is leading the children down the wrong path. We need to strengthen our walk with the Lord so that our children can have a godly leader in their life.

Parent/step-parent role is confusing and difficult to manage at times. When our roles are not clear, we find ourselves hanging on by a thread. But, what we CAN do is continue to instill the principles given to us in the Bible.

When Satan tries to take your child's innocence, fight him with scripture, prayer, and extra time with God. Do you know what Satan hates? He hates it when you try to make things work out between all the parents. He hates to see teamwork! He despises the joy that comes from our trials. So, let's kick Satan to the curb and show him what God can do in our messiest situations.

Thoughts for today:

1. Fill in the blank. When faced with difficult situations with my kids/step-kids I react by

   _____

   _____

   _____

2. When my kids/step-kids come to me with problems related to their other parent I

usually:

a. listen

b. get upset

c. don't want to get involved

3. What is my relationship like with all other parents involved? Am I actively trying to get along or am I adding fuel to the fire? Am I trying to discuss important issues that come up or am I just venting my frustrations but not really dealing with the issues?

    _____

    _____

    _____

    _____

    _____

    _____

4.   If you are stuck in a situation that feels hopeless, turn to God. There are many circumstances that we won't be able to work it out between us, but God can. It's time to remember our place. We need to support and love and guide. God will handle the unwanted behaviors from others. God wants the best for your kids and He will handle it. We need to be patient and wait on Him.

Prayer:

Lord, you know the fear that surrounds me when the kids have to deal with such big issues when they are away. I want them to know and understand the "why" behind living with such high standards. I want the kids to have the desire to live godly lives. Help me Lord! I can only do this with You! Please take my attitude out of the picture and fill me with Your love! Help me to raise the kids in love and know how to conquer these battles we are facing. I'm so thankful for Your peace in the storm. I am grateful that You think I am a capable parent and able to raise the children the best way I know how. Please help us deal with each situation as it comes. Help us not to feel overwhelmed or lonely. Help my spouse and I to be a team! Thank you for what You are about to do in our lives! Amen!

DAY 28 - THE UNTOLD STORY

Psalm 71:15-21

My mouth will tell of your righteous deeds, of your saving acts all day long—though I know not how to relate them all. I will come and proclaim your mighty acts, Sovereign Lord; I will proclaim your righteous deeds, yours alone. Since my youth, God, you have taught me, and to this day I declare your marvelous deeds. Even when I am old and gray, do not forsake me, my God, till I declare your power to the next generation, your mighty acts to all who are to come. Your righteousness, God, reaches to the heavens, you who have done great things. Who is like you, God? Though you have made me see troubles, many and bitter, you will restore my life again; from the depths of the earth you will again bring me up. You will increase my honor and comfort me once more.

I always knew there would come a day when my

girls would ask me what happened between their father and me. A couple of weeks ago we were driving to church. I had noticed that my daughter had been asking some different types of questions that day since coming home from school. She asked me if her father was my "ex" and I said "yes" and explained what that meant. Then came the question I knew she would eventually ask, "Why are you and daddy not married anymore?"

Luckily, I had prepared myself for this question. Had she asked me this a few years ago, I probably would not have been in a good position to discuss this. It took me years to be able to think this through. I didn't want to make a huge mistake and scar my children with information they simply did not need to know.

I had made the decision that I would always answer any questions they may have, but not in a way that is demeaning or degrading to another. So, there I sat driving to church (when most interesting topics come up) and the thoughts just flooded my mind.

I wasn't going to lie to her, but I didn't feel she was at an age to understand the situation. I said a quick prayer for God to guide my words.

Obviously, I didn't answer her question quick enough because she asked me again. "Mommy, why are you and daddy not married?" I opened my mouth to speak, but it seemed that words would not come. I honestly wished I could just change the subject, but this eight year old is too quick for that!

I explained to Hailey and Avery that when they were very little that something happened between their father and me. I said that it was not a good situation and that I took them to live with Mimi and Papaw.

I explained that sometimes people can make choices that affect other people's lives and when people are married any decision we make can affect the other person. I know this sounds so vague, but that was my intention.

I guess this was enough of an answer for her because she then hopped to other questions. I was thankful. Let me give you an example of why I feel protecting your kids from unneeded information is important.

Divorce is not a happy memory. It's not something that we should take lightly. It's a time of brokenness, pain, and anger. I heard a story recently about a man who was wanting to find out why his parents divorced. He went to his parents and asked each one the same question...why?

His mom would not give up the details, but told him the same reason she always did. The dad gave in to the son's persistence and shared way too much detail. Now, the man is struggling to even have a relationship with his parents due to the painful information he received from his dad. He is struggling to cope with what he learned and can't even comprehend it all.

Why burden our children with something so painful? It's one thing to give them a simple explanation when they are an adult and can understand, but it's another thing to give such intricate details that they can't get the thought out of their heads!

It's not a secret what happened in my marriage.

151

As I said before, I grew up in the "glass house" since my dad was a pastor. I've always been an open person with my life. I can share my story with others when the time is right.

In my past, I've almost felt like I "had" to share my life's story just so people wouldn't judge me for being divorced. I no longer feel this way. It's taken me years to feel "ok" with my life and my past.

One day, when my girls are old enough and they want to know the story, I will tell them. I will tell them that Satan sends temptations to people in so many ways. We choose our actions. People make mistakes. Sometimes those mistakes lead to a break up in a marriage.

In our case, it was adultery. It happens so often. Some marriages can withstand it and some don't make it. I would have loved to say that I was able to work it out, but I can't say that. Some days I wonder "what if I did stay?" or "what if I had responded differently?"

I tell my husband all the time that I wouldn't wish divorce on anyone. If there had been a way that I thought I could have handled the pain of abandonment and betrayal, I would have. I've had so many friends that have survived adultery in their marriages. It's hard not to judge yourself sometimes for feeling like a failure when you see others make it through.

However, God has already forgiven us for our failures. He casts our past sins far away and never looks at them again. What an awesome God we serve that can give us such grace! This is the God I serve! He will guide me and direct me. He will give me the wisdom when speaking to my kids about such sensitive issues.

I pray today that you will also consider your words when sharing with your children. Consider the damage you can do! Let's let God handle this in His timing.

Thoughts for today:

1. Have your kids been asking about your past marriage? What have you told them? What if they were to ask? Have you thought this through?

_____

_____

_____

_____

_____

2. How have you coped with your past marriage? Are you still holding on to a grudge from years ago? Have you come to a place of forgiveness?

_____

_____

_____

_____

_____

_____

3. We all make mistakes. However, let's try to protect our children from the unnecessary pains that could be created with our words. Let's not purposefully speak hateful words because of deep-seated anger. It's time to start digging through all of the hurts from the past. Allow God to take

each pain from you and replace it with His peace and joy today.

Prayer:

Lord, you know my heart. You know that I could easily share the details that surrounded my past. I don't ever want to hurt my children or their relationship with their other parent. Please help me to be self-controlled when I am faced with questions. Please give me the words to explain without need for painful memories. I want to protect and guide my children and show them what You have done in my life regardless of past mistakes or failures. I am so thankful for Your grace and mercy. I am thankful for Your strength that brought me through such a hard time in my life. Thank you for never leaving me, Lord! Amen!

DAY 29 - BATTLE WOUNDS

James 1:2-5 Consider it pure joy, my brothers and sisters, whenever you face trials of many kinds, because you know that the testing of your faith produces perseverance. Let perseverance finish its work so that you may be mature and complete, not lacking anything. If any of you lacks wisdom, you should ask God, who gives generously to all without finding fault, and it will be given to you.

I think we can all agree that God doesn't promote divorce. It's not the ideal situation for anyone or any child for that matter. However, I can tell you today that I am a stronger person for going through this trial in my life. I will never look at someone the same way who has, or is currently struggling with, the same serious issues that I have dealt with. I've learned to be a more compassionate person through my own struggles.

This doesn't mean "I've made it" or that I will

ever be "ok" with the fact that this is real and this is my life. I think if I was so nonchalant about the entire event then it wouldn't say much about my character. If I am going to be real with you, then you will know by my words that this was the hardest time in my life. It still plagues me in some ways today.

I never wanted to share my children. I never wanted to have an open wound that seems to be a constant reminder at times. I never wanted anyone to look at me and wonder "what must she have done wrong" or give me a label for the rest of my life. I never wanted my kids to grow up having to deal with this or ask me why their parents are no longer together. This was never the life I pictured.

In the same way, God knew. God knew my every breath before I even took it. He knew how my life would continue to unfold. No matter what I have been faced with or what the future may hold, I cling to the One who holds my every moment. A while back I laid my hurts, bitterness, and anger at Christ's feet. Yes, I still struggle. I am HUMAN! :)

But, through all my storms I still have such a big hope for my life! God is my life! He is my hope! He is my future! I want you all to know today that there is a LIGHT at the end of the darkness. His name is Jesus! He desires for you to come to him with all your hurts and heartaches. He gave His life for you!

He wants you to draw near to him today and find that peace that I have. I have such a great joy and peace from the Lord. I am continually reminded of this through his scriptures in the

Bible.

I'm praying today that you have this relationship with the One who created you! No matter what you have been through and no matter what you have done, He is waiting for you to call on him today.

Thoughts for today:

1. What have you learned during this time reading?

_____
_____
_____

2. How has God changed you?

_____
_____
_____
_____
_____

3. What areas will you continue to work on in your own life?

_____
_____
_____
_____
_____

Prayer:

Lord, I pray today that you will use me. I thank you for allowing me to overcome my hardships. Thank you for your grace and forgiveness! Lord, I want you to use my life. I want you to pour your love into my family. I need your guidance throughout my journey here on earth. I can't do this alone. I know that life will not always be easy, but I know you will be by my side. I'm so comforted to know you are holding my hand! I'm ready, God! Let's do this! Amen.

DAY 30 BE ENCOURAGED

Romans 15:5-6 May the God who gives endurance and encouragement give you the same attitude of mind toward each other that Christ Jesus had, so that with one mind and one voice you may glorify the God and Father of our Lord Jesus Christ.

Sometimes, people (including ourselves) feel like the ones who should lead a church or have more impact on souls are the ones without a past they are afraid to share. We feel like people who have stayed on the straight and narrow would be better at "directing the flock." How wrong we have it!

If you read the Bible, you will see that God used the poor, needy, broken, and wounded. Every story I've read shows the "real life" of people back in those days. Why should it be different today? Why do we feel like God can't use us because we have scars? Why are we incapable or fearful of telling the truth of our past?

159

If you have faith in the Lord, it's time to take a bold step. Until we start to be honest with people, we will never experience the freedom from our past in Christ! God gives perfect peace. We can't find that anywhere else. You can search all you want, have all the money, all the cars, great jobs, beauty, and popularity, but you will still never find true happiness and peace.

Sometimes, after talking with someone, I feel more bruised than before the conversation began. Finding myself today in a pastor's wife position makes me want to be even more protective. I'm super protective over my husband and children. Woe be to the one who hurts my family!

But it's true, I don't want to bring anymore judgment or attention to something in my past that I finally am over! However, that's not how God has led me. He made it very clear for me to share my heart with others, no matter how uncomfortable it may be.

So, what about you? Why not find the freedom from your past today! It's so tiring trying to pretend nothing happened. I know! There was a time in my life that I didn't want to remember.

Now, God has used those painful memories and is working in my heart and my life to be more passionate about sharing. It's time we quit thinking these people in the Bible are simply fictional characters. They were real people living with the same issues we face today.

I also want to speak to those today who do not have scars from your past. Check your heart and ask God to give you a sensitive and compassionate spirit to those who have been broken. I didn't have this before.

I've been there, but you can't ever say "that won't ever happen to me or my family!" I am a living testimony to that concept. I said never, and here I am living through the same situations I spoke of. Let's all learn to love like Christ did. He is our ultimate example.

Thoughts for today:

1. When Satan tries to tell you that you are nothing, remember that God gave His life for you and you are His treasure!

2. When you feel insecure about sharing your life with others, remember that God will give you the boldness. He was not ashamed or afraid to be different! Ask God for confidence and trust Him! I promise you that obedience to God is so rewarding!!

3. Remember that no matter what others may think, we answer to God. He is our biggest cheerleader! Don't let comments from others bring you down. Live for God. Resist the devil!

Prayer:

Lord, please don't let me waste my life trying to hide who I am! Please give me the confidence and wisdom I need to share my life and testimony with others. Let your Holy Spirit guide me when the time is right. Help to be an encouragement to others and not a stumbling block. I love you,

Lord. I want to be obedient!!! Amen!

DEAR READER:

Steve and I would love to hear from you and be available to minister to you, your church, or a small group. We feel like there is a huge need for ministry when it comes to blended families.

If you would like to contact us for a ministry need, please feel free to email us at: brokentoblendedministries@gmail.com

Please be in prayer as God continues to lead us in future projects for churches and couples. We look forward to great things!

Steve and Samara Ashley

Made in the USA
Columbia, SC
30 April 2017